Effort and Excellence in Urban Classrooms

Critical Issues in Educational Leadership Series

Joseph Murphy, Series Editor

Effort and Excellence in Urban Classrooms:
Expecting—and Getting—Success with All Students
DICK CORBETT, BRUCE WILSON, AND BELINDA WILLIAMS

Developing Educational Leaders: A Working Model:
The Learning Community in Action
CYNTHIA J. NORRIS, BRUCE G. BARNETT,
MARGARET R. BASOM, AND DIANE M. YERKES

Understanding and Assessing the Charter School Movement
JOSEPH MURPHY AND CATHERINE DUNN SHIFFMAN

School Choice in Urban America:
Magnet Schools and the Pursuit of Equity
CLAIRE SMREKAR AND ELLEN GOLDRING

Lessons from High-Performing Hispanic Schools:
Creating Learning Communities
PEDRO REYES, JAY D. SCRIBNER, AND
ALICIA PAREDES SCRIBNER, EDS.

Schools for Sale: Why Free Market Policies
Won't Improve America's Schools, and What Will
ERNEST R. HOUSE

Reclaiming Educational Administration as a Caring Profession
LYNN G. BECK

Effort and Excellence in Urban Classrooms

EXPECTING—AND GETTING—SUCCESS WITH ALL STUDENTS

Dick Corbett, Bruce Wilson, & Belinda Williams

Teachers College
Columbia University
New York and London

NEA Professional Library
National Education Association
Washington, D.C.

Published simultaneously by Teachers College Press, 1234 Amsterdam Avenue, New York, NY 10027 and the NEA Professional Library, 1201 16th Street N.W., Washington, D.C. 20036

This book was supported by a grant from the Office of Educational Research and Improvement, U.S. Department of Education. The opinions expressed are those of the authors and do not represent the policy of the U.S. Department of Education.

Library of Congress Cataloging-in-Publication Data

Corbett, H. Dickson, 1950–
    Effort and excellence in urban classrooms : expecting—and getting—success with all students / Dick Corbett, Bruce Wilson & Belinda Williams.
        p. cm.
    Includes bibliographical references.
    ISBN 0-8077-4216-3 (pbk. : alk. paper)—ISBN 0-8077-4217-1 (cloth : alk. paper)
        1. Education, Urban—United States.   2. Academic achievement—United States.
    3. Effective teaching—United States.   I. Wilson, Bruce L.   II. Williams, Belinda.
    III. Title.

    LC5131 .C62   2002
    370′.9173′2—dc21   2001060366

ISBN 0-8077-4216-3 (paper)
ISBN 0-8077-4217-1 (cloth)

Printed on acid-free paper
Manufactured in the United States of America

09 08 07 06 05 04 03   8 7 6 5 4 3 2

Contents

Acknowledgments

Several thoughtful and inspiring educators read portions of this manuscript. Their comments and their commitment to making schools better places for all children enriched us, and our work, immeasurably. Our thanks, therefore, to Brian Driscoll, William Franklin, Steve Hoelscher, Sarah Isham, Mike Knapp, Troy Regis, Grace Stanford, Eileen Lymus Swerdlick, and Emma Terry.

We also express our appreciation to Susan Talley of the Office of Educational Research and Improvement, U.S. Department of Education, for not only guiding us through the administrative side of our field-initiated studies grant but also for taking such a productive interest in the substantive side.

Finally, we dedicate this work to Bob Williams: husband, father, and friend.

Effort and Excellence in Urban Classrooms

1

Overview

The purpose of the research on which this book is based was to examine urban teachers' assumptions about the capabilities of low-income students as learners and how these assumptions influenced both classroom instructional activities and student performance. Our expectation was that teachers would vary considerably in the ways they defined and acted on low-income students' strengths and weaknesses and that investigating the effects of these pedagogical differences would yield important insights into the well-documented achievement gap between poor students and their wealthier counterparts.

During our study's 3 years, we combined survey, interview, and classroom observation data-collection techniques to enable us to probe both the depth and breadth of the role such assumptions played in two small-city school districts. Both districts served diverse student populations whose academic performance reflected the prevailing national test score discrepancies among various income groups. Both were actively addressing this achievement gap and thus were willing to cooperate with any research project that might shed light on the situation.

We found that most educators in the two districts espoused the belief that "all children can learn and succeed in school" but that this phrase had multiple meanings, at least three of which appeared to have profound effects on what went on in school. The different meanings became clear in the qualifiers that people attached to the core statement. Two were related, with one qualifier being "if their parents support education" and the other "if the students put forth the effort." Both clearly established limits in educators' assessments of their ability to contribute to student success. Even though nearly all the people we talked to and observed who expressed these beliefs proved to be highly committed to helping students and keenly interested in using instructional practices well suited to their situations, they eventually accepted that there was only so much they could do and that some students simply would not succeed.

The third qualifier was "and it's my job to make sure that they

1

do." Educators making this statement refused to allow home situations and/or student motivation to serve as reasons why students failed. Instead, they expected all students to complete their work successfully and prodded the children until they did. We labeled this an "It's my job" or "No excuses" belief, using the phrases as synonyms to refer to a way of thinking that acknowledged the challenges of educating low-income students but did not see those challenges as insurmountable.

Veteran educators might distinguish the first two qualifiers as "realistic and inevitable" and the latter as "idealistic and unsustainable." We would be so inclined as well, except that we saw this belief unwaveringly enacted in classrooms; and our conversations with teachers and students in those classrooms proved that they resolutely believed that their efforts dramatically reduced the chances of students' falling through the historically huge academic cracks in the classroom floors of high-poverty schools. Certainly a sizable number of students on the path to poor performance claimed to have been redirected, as the following chapters detail.

Lest there be any misunderstanding, we must make clear that "No excuses" and "It's my job" were not simply interchangeable rhetorical rallying cries for the educators we studied. They had no intention of allowing their indelible commitment to low-income students' academic success to be reduced to the easily-said-but-rarely-acted-on-seriously status of the omnipresent "All children can learn." They certainly believed this—and that all children could learn at high levels. But these beliefs were not merely noble aspirations; for these educators, they were practical, self-imposed mandates.

We also need to underline the point that the teachers and schools described in this book were not trying to push their students to master basic skills or to attain some level of minimal competence. Not at all. Nor did they take pride when their students compared favorably to those who attended other schools that served families of similar socioeconomic status. Not a chance. Instead, these educators were determined to enable these children to be competitive academically *with anyone*. Effort *and* excellence were their goals, and jointly these two terms comprised their definition of student success. Thus they did not assume that the students' unequal starting points equated to unequal abilities to achieve.

This latter group of teachers focused on what students could do, not on what they could not do. That is, their students' existing strengths became the foundation for building success in the classroom. The teachers also accepted that they had control only over what went on in school. Student success, then, was going to have to be attained during the schoolday.

Whether this latter group of teachers knew it or not—and most indicated to us that their actions were born of experience-based conviction as much as research—this willingness to find classroom solutions to achievement differences had growing support in studies on student learning and closing the achievement gap in low-income schools. We venture briefly into this research at this point only to highlight the fact that these teachers' "common sense" and empirical findings were not far apart. In the last chapter of the book, we more thoroughly situate our findings within the current research context.

Because of their districts' demographics, all the teachers who worked in them (regardless of the qualifications they made to the "All children can succeed" belief) were well aware of the achievement differences among the students they served. There was little comfort to be found in the fact that the large gap between the academic performance of majority children and poor urban children was a nationally stubborn one (Hedges & Howell, 1999).

Indeed, the national debate about the reasons for this gap continues to rage intensively. For a long while, participants in the discussion concentrated mostly on factors beyond schools' control. Fortunately, a thoughtful piece on the topic has put that unproductive exercise to rest.

Jencks and Phillips (1998) argue convincingly that students' experiences in classrooms offer much more fertile ground to plow for solutions than heredity or poverty or some other deficit lurking in a child's background. The authors suggest that instead of looking at students' inadequacies as the sources of the gap, educators, researchers, and policy makers alike should attend more keenly to how these children are taught. In other words, Jencks and Phillips say that the academic failures of children who traditionally have not done well in school may be due more to inadequate instructional practices (such as a using a traditional curriculum or emphasizing a narrow range of intelligences) and policies (e.g., tracking and standardized assessments) than to the effects of poverty.

Still, the gap is pervasive. Both the popular and educational presses recount numerous instances of district, state, and national tests showing that most poor schools do poorly. The bombardment of these messages about failure in low-income schools is unrelenting. Worse, the "bad news" reinforces a "cultural-deficit" argument for students' woeful performance that can only conclude that students, and their backgrounds, are the problem.

How, then, could the educators we mentioned above hold steadfast to their optimism? Were their ambitions no more than admirable but impotent cheerleading in the face of an overwhelming academic mismatch? Or were their intuitions sound and worthy of being the foundation for subsequent student success?

Actually, the research is on their side. Studies of intelligence, learning, and instruction now reject conceptions of low-income learners as inherently culturally deprived, lacking in ability, unmotivated, and at risk. Instead, research shows that it is much more productive for educators to regard such students as culturally diverse, capable, motivated, and resilient (Williams, 1996).

For example, all children bring specific cultural knowledge and experiences with them to school, regardless of their background. Research suggests that teachers should connect with this knowledge and these experiences with relevant instructional materials to best facilitate intellectual growth (Knapp, Shields, & Turnbull, 1995; Prawat, 1993). To do this requires that educators value and access the diverse environments within which their students live and build bridges between the home and school. Labeling children from low-income environments as educationally disadvantaged or at risk blinds educators to the various natural talents that each possesses. Thus, as Deschenes, Tyack, and Cuban (2001) suggest, schools would better serve these students if staff focused on how to adapt the school to students rather than how to force students to fit into a rather narrowly defined mainstream of academic behavior and performance.

In another significant strand of research, Gardner (1983) debunked the idea that intelligence is a unitary concept, thereby challenging educators to identify and teach to the multiple intelligences represented in their classrooms. Too often pedagogy rewards only a few forms of ability and even fewer means of expressing that ability to the detriment of children whose strengths reside outside of those narrow boundaries. The consequence, then, is that educators interpret low-income students' poor academic performance as inevitable, which sets in motion a debilitating spiral of failure that can only result in a child's giving up.

On the other hand, research shows that success breeds the motivation to succeed. This generalization is as true for low-income as high-income students. Despite the inside- and outside-school obstacles low-income students face, the astounding aspect about these children is that so many of them are competent, responsible, productive, and healthy individuals (Winfield, 1991). This resilience gives educators cognizant of how to nurture it a firm foothold from which to boost these students to higher levels of achievement.

Whether intentionally or intuitively, the educators in the two districts we studied who accepted the responsibility of ensuring student success did so convinced of the academic strengths of their students. They saw their students as richly diverse, capable, motivated (or able to become so), and resilient, and the teachers' pedagogy proceeded from this premise. The teachers took the premise one step further, however. Because they knew the students could succeed, they took it upon themselves to make sure that success happened.

The adherents to this "It's our job" philosophy were not blind to poverty. They knew that their students faced some large obstacles to gaining ground on wealthier students. As research has shown, the cultural capital and educational resources that students possess outside of school tremendously influence their performance in school (e.g., Roscigno & Ainsworth-Darnell, 1999). What these educators decided was that poverty should not automatically resign children to low levels of academic performance and that differences in the mix of intelligences a student possessed were individual differences, not socioeconomic or racial ones. Based on this understanding, the people described in the following pages viewed it as their responsibility to provide the kinds of opportunities their students needed to succeed.

We attempt to explain in the remainder of this book why educators made this decision, how they acted on it, and the effects that it had on students. In doing so, we hope to add weight to the argument that assuming all students are capable of succeeding in school and accepting nothing short of this outcome are promising, though strenuous, components of an approach for finally closing the achievement gap in this country.

ABOUT THE STUDY

The two districts chosen for this research included a small Midwestern city and a comparably sized city on the Eastern seaboard located on the outskirts of a major metropolitan area. These districts were selected for two reasons. First, we wanted to work in settings with many of the same demographic characteristics of large-city schools but without the complicated trappings of large bureaucracies. Each district had more than ten elementary schools and four middle schools or junior highs; one had a single high school while the other had two. The student enrollments in each were around 10,000 and contained sizable proportions of poor students. The smaller midwestern district reported just over half of their students as eligible for free or reduced-price lunch while the East Coast district provided similar services to 29% of their students. Individual schools within the districts varied considerably in this regard. Although the districts were not overwhelmingly poor, we decided that examining teachers' assumptions about the relationship between income and learning would be particularly rich in settings where teachers saw very diverse students daily.

Second, we felt the environment for looking at these beliefs would be enriched in districts that acknowledged an achievement gap between poorer students and wealthier ones. Both districts not only formally recognized this through the creation of local task forces and mission statements but also had implemented programs to reduce that gap.

The districts also worked with the local business community in designing and funding special programs. In the case of the Midwestern district, the major area employer was a large international corporation that had a long history of providing extra support for education. The East Coast district had a more diversified economy and drew on a range of local corporations to support improvement initiatives.

Our research was not intended to "evaluate" any of these programs; we and district administrators described it as what it was—an effort to look at how teachers' assumptions about their students' learning capabilities played out in the classroom. We willingly shared with educators in the districts our general findings about the different meanings of "All children can learn and succeed" and the kinds of actions teachers adhering to the "It's my job"/"No excuses" belief took in the classroom, without making any specific references to individuals or schools. Such feedback mostly occurred informally as people inquired about what we were learning. As happens in so many school districts, very few of the district officials with whom we originally discussed our research were still working there by the study's end.

We began this work expecting that the beliefs teachers held about students' learning capabilities would have a powerful and direct impact on their daily actions in the classroom and that these actions, in turn, would significantly influence the success of their students. We were not sure, however, how these assumptions and actions might actually play out in reality. Thus we relied on a mix of methodological approaches.

In the first year we started by observing district professional development activities and school improvement committee meetings to help sensitize us to the range of assumptions prevalent among teachers, administrators, and community members. From that experience we chose to interview and observe more than 50 classroom teachers representative of the range of experience, subject matter, and grade level in the districts. In conjunction with those classroom visits, we also talked to 200 students about their classroom experiences. Finally, we expanded on some of the highlights from these initial conversations and observations with a survey of 1,079 teachers and 974 parents in the two districts.

The first year of data collection confirmed that most teachers subscribed to the belief that "All children can learn and succeed" but that there were important qualifiers that teachers attached to this core statement, as mentioned earlier. Because parents indicated that they believed more strongly in their children's learning capabilities than they thought the teachers' did, we found it useful to juxtapose parents' responses with teachers' in our analysis of the adults' varying beliefs about student learning.

In the second year we wanted to learn more about what people meant by their qualifiers and what the implications might be for student learning. We therefore conducted interviews with 125 teachers in the two districts to explore the different meanings they attached to the generic belief statement. From these conversations we identified specific classrooms where we thought an "It's my job" philosophy might be enacted. We observed those classrooms and talked with students about their experiences.

After examining this philosophy in action at the classroom level, we wanted to see if we could identify whole schools that enacted it. Initially, we visited nearly every school in the Eastern city and the six poorest ones in the Midwestern one. In both cases, this was what the superintendents preferred us to do. Over time, we happened to find one school in each district where nearly all of the educators espoused nearly similar beliefs about their obligation and efficacy in enabling students to do their work and do it well. That is, the "It's my job" and "No excuses" terminology appeared in the language of nearly everyone in the buildings. We devoted more time to these in the latter stages of the research to better understand how such a philosophy originated and spread. During the third year, then, we observed meetings, watched programs in action, and interviewed staff, parents, and students.

All the other schools also had teachers who accepted no excuses for failure, but they operated singly or in "pockets" within their buildings. Thus our decisions about where to spend our time depended on the extent to which the guiding principle in a building was "It's my job"/"No excuses."

ORGANIZATION OF THE BOOK

In the following pages, we examine what the "It's my job"/"No excuses" philosophy meant in thought and action. We provide in-depth looks into classrooms and schools where the residents portrayed what the path to academic success for all actually looked and sounded like. Along the way, we offer substantial evidence that educators' acceptance of the responsibility for student success might be a potentially powerful influence on closing the achievement gap.

In Chapter 2, we illustrate the different meanings that educators and parents in the two districts attached to the phrase "All children can learn and succeed." Variations of this statement have become obligatory inclusions in nearly every educational agency's mission statement and in most important pieces of educational legislation in the last 10 years. Its use is well intended, an exhortation to attend to traditionally underserved populations. Its simple appearance is deceptive, however, because we have found that in the minds of many educators it is only a stem, a prompt if you will, to which several significantly different qualifiers become attached.

Chapter 3 addresses the issue of the parental role in education. Our argument is that schools adopting a philosophy that asserted that there were no fatal obstacles to working effectively with low-income students did not use the lack of parental support as a valid explanation for student failure. Instead, they celebrated any positive parent influence as "enriching" what went on at school. This argument has a tough row to hoe, however, in high-poverty situations. Thus this chapter looks at home versus school issues from the perspectives of both those at home and those at school. Its somewhat surprising finding is that the parents in our two districts attributed their struggles in promoting academic success with their children to the lack of effort and interest of educators—just as many educators did with the parents.

Chapter 4 begins a three-chapter journey into classrooms and schools that were demonstrably enabling students who traditionally had done poorly in school to perform at high academic levels. Chapter 4 looks inside classrooms occupied by teachers who adhered fervently to the belief that it was their job to supply the encouragement and support necessary for their charges to do well. The text uses individual lessons as the springboards to describe how four teachers—two from elementary schools and one each from a junior high and high school— promoted high achievement among habitually low-performing students.

The effort that the above teachers put into their work set a high standard, perhaps one that others around them saw as impossible to attain or to maintain for very long. At least the four, according to students, were exceptions in their buildings. Apparently, without the encouragement and support analogous to what "It's my job"–believing teachers gave to their students, other teachers were no more likely to achieve excellence continually and consistently than were children. Thus Chapters 5 and 6 move to the school level and introduce the reader to two faculties whose shared purposes and ways of organizing themselves assisted most of the teachers in enabling all of their children to succeed—with the same types of students with whom other schools in their respective districts had not been so effective.

Chapter 7 steps back from the schools to state what we think was going on in these settings that raised the academic performance of all students. Quite simply, the teachers and schools refused to accept any excuses for students' performing poorly in school. Instead, they took it upon themselves as their jobs to supply all the support necessary for students to complete assignments at an acceptable level of quality. We argue that there was no recipe for doing this and adamantly avoid extracting any categories of actions and/or programs that would promote success for all. Instead, in the settings we studied, "It's our job" and "No excuses" were catchwords for a belief, one that infused every action educators took and was the sole criterion they used to determine what and how they should teach their students.

Finally, Chapter 8 highlights the kinds of support and policies we think are needed to promote the efforts of schools that shoulder the burden for student success. This chapter strays a bit from our data, by necessity. As we stated, we were able to identify only one such school in each of the two districts we studied. Thus we could identify no districtwide support and/or policies that reinforced the "It's my job"/ "No excuses" philosophy. For the most part, schools were free to determine their own fates. This chapter, then, asks the question: What can be done to encourage, nurture, and maintain schools that determinedly act on the belief that all children can and will succeed in school?

A NOTE ON USAGE

As our research was ending and without knowledge of our findings, a national campaign adopting the slogan of "No Excuses" was launched by the Heritage Foundation. Normally associated with advocating conservative policies for education, the foundation sought to create public support for "better education for the poor" (Carter, 1999, p. ii). The foundation acknowledged that "liberals, centrists, and conservatives" may differ vehemently on the specifics of a political agenda for education but hoped that all could unite in the belief that "there is no excuse for the academic failure of most public schools serving poor children" (Carter, 1999, p. ii). The foundation's own research concentrated on principals in "high-performing, high-poverty schools" and identified how these leaders shaped schools to better serve their traditionally underachieving student populations. Each principal's actions are illustrated fully in *No Excuses: Seven Principals of Low-Income Schools Who Set the Standard for High Achievement* (Carter, 1999).

We mention this only to acknowledge that the phrase "No excuses" is now well established in the public domain. Our usage of it differs significantly from the Heritage Foundation's, especially in so far as (1) we attribute this belief to teachers rather than principals; (2) teachers explained the belief as applying to their approach to working with low-income students rather than as a slogan for a nation to apply to the prospects for success in low-income schools; and (3) teachers' definitions of "success" encompassed a host of indicators that reflected both effort and excellence, not just test scores.

We use the phrases "No excuses" and "It's my job" interchangeably to refer to teachers' belief that they have to assume responsibility for whether children succeed in school. We considered forgoing our long-standing use of the former because of the potential for our work to be confused with that of the Heritage Foundation. However, it conveys concisely what a number of educators adamantly maintained: A teacher can accept no excuses for the failure of his or her students.

We use pseudonyms for all references to teachers, students, and schools. We also stick to their grammar, syntax, and word usage in quotes. At times, as educators in the districts read drafts of the text, they expressed some concern, particularly about how their students sounded in print. They worried that the language might reflect poorly on both the children's effort and excellence. Others thought that the verbatim quotes lent "authority" to what the students said. We sided with the latter.

THE ACHIEVEMENT GAP AND SCHOOLS THAT WORK
FOR ALL STUDENTS

We want to end this chapter by making clear that we are not describing schools where performance indicators for low-income students were only in an up-trend. Such indications may be worth noting, but unless the gap between these students' performance and that of their wealthier peers was also growing narrower, then the relative academic positions of the two groups would remain unchanged and low-income students would endure the same educational disadvantages that accrue to poor performance that they had always encountered. On the other hand, all students have to make academic progress, otherwise the lower achievers' success would only stem from a lowered bar. In other words, we will highlight in this book those teachers and schools that achieved equity *and* excellence.

2

The Different Meanings of "All Children Can Succeed"

An interesting discovery from the more than 1,000 surveys and several hundred interviews we conducted with administrators, teachers, students, and parents was that the signature reform slogan "All children can succeed" had become openly acknowledged as an acceptable and valid statement of fact. This was perhaps a predictable development, given the omnipresence of the phrase in schools' and districts' mission and vision statements. Still, the majority of people we talked with affirmed the obligation of public schools to attend assiduously to all students, especially the traditionally underserved.

However, as people talked further in interviews or extended their survey responses with written comments, important distinctions emerged in their interpretations of the phrase's meaning. In this chapter, we elaborate on these. We do so not for the intellectual exercise of splitting hairs about esoteric semantic differences but rather to suggest that these beliefs had practical implications for what happened in the classrooms we studied and how likely it was that the achievement gap among groups of students in the two districts could be eradicated.

What we heard and read were differences about where the responsibility for ensuring student success should be lodged. Some respondents said that all students could succeed and it was the teachers' job to ensure that this happened. In other words, they did not want educators to accept any excuses for learning's not taking place. We have labeled this a "No excuses" or "It's my job" belief. Others took exception to such an idealistic philosophy, suggesting that there were limits to what educators could accomplish. One portion maintained that students had to show some effort first; another group stressed that home environments had to be more supportive of education.

Below we use a host of quotes to illustrate these differences. The reader should keep in mind that all the people quoted below directly stated that they believed that all students could succeed in school. This chapter concentrates on this group because it is significant to us that the people who were apparently the most optimistic about the prospects for students who traditionally did poorly in school proffered such varied meanings to the slogan they espoused, and many of them set limits on what they could accomplish in the classroom. Thus even the ostensible "best cases" saw considerable obstacles to educating the underserved.

It is, of course, possible that a number of these educators simply parroted what they perceived to be an educationally correct response. We had no way of judging their sincerity in that respect, except in those instances when we also were able to sit in on their classes. However, the fact that a sizable proportion of these teachers qualified the applicability of the phrase suggests that merely infusing a school's or district's mission statement with some version of "All children can succeed" has little practical value. Only extended dialogue about the actual meaning of the statement is likely to move it from rhetoric to reality.

ALL CHILDREN CAN SUCCEED—AND IT'S EDUCATORS' RESPONSIBILITY TO SEE THAT THEY DO

A portion of study participants refused to venture excuses for their not being successful with all students. As teachers and parents philosophized about working with and raising the achievement levels of traditionally low-performing students, we repeatedly heard from this segment that all students could do the work they were given in class. Four teachers, ranging across the spectrum of grades, summed up the argument. The first two emphasized the importance of not qualifying one's belief in students' learning capabilities, noting the presence of the word *but* as a tip-off that perhaps someone really did not think that all of his or her students could succeed:

> My philosophy is that "All students can learn," not "All can learn *but* . . . !" The key is giving enough time and support. That support has to be during the schoolday.

> I have never had a kid who didn't want to learn. I have some with limited ability, but it is my job to make sure learning happens. If you let "buts" creep in, you get built-in excuses for why they don't learn. But kids can still do it. For example, I remember one student who was abused as a child who still remembers her school experiences as those that turned her around. There is

a book written about her. If she could do it, it's peanuts for anyone else to do.

The second two teachers picked up on another thread from the first
two quotes—that creating a success-promoting environment *in the
classroom* is possible:

> All students can master the work, given the time and support to
> do it.

> While I agree that prior knowledge and motivation vary greatly
> from student to student, I believe all students can learn given the
> proper environment and teaching strategies in my classroom. It
> is a challenge, but we can make a difference.

Teachers in this category were not blind to student differences.
They acknowledged that students brought varying skills and learning
styles to the classroom. However, they did not subsequently infer that
those differences reflected a student's innate capabilities. Three teachers exemplified this refusal to connect current performance with inherited ability:

> I don't feel anyone lacks ability. They just have ability that is
> as of yet untapped. The right approach could unlock doors.

> They learn and master skills outside of school all the time.
> They can accomplish the same in a school setting also.

> All students can make progress. They just begin their journey
> at different places and continue at different paces.

Teachers argued that it was more productive to assume that students varied in the ways that they were "smart" and that teachers
should factor these individual differences into their instructional plans:

> I definitely believe it is my job to make it happen. It is my job to
> draw out students. That is why multiple intelligences is so im-
> portant. We need to draw out their gifts. My job is to impart and

get it out of them. It is important to start where they are and bring them to the next level. That is the foundation of my philosophy.

Acting on such beliefs required teachers to accept that the starting point for learning was the teacher's adeptness at understanding and accommodating each student's particular circumstances. Teachers' recognition of students' needs was the prelude to preventing students' failure in the classroom, as one teacher explained:

> It is actually embarrassing to listen to the excuse that teachers give at district meetings. I think in some cases it is adults who are not willing. If all the buildings would do what is being done at [our school], we wouldn't have the problems we do. It's not because of the kids, but rather because some people don't understand or don't want to understand kids.

Teachers maintained that needs recognition, then, had to serve as the basis for action. At a minimum, the school had to adjust various practices. These adaptations included the curriculum at a student's grade level:

> I agree with the view that all students can learn. We don't all learn at the same pace. We need to make accommodations at the second grade and fill in the gaps. It is my job to fill in the gaps. I see it as meeting a need. You need to make sure they have materials so that they can feel success.

Teachers also adapted their instructional strategies:

> I have some kids believing it is their responsibility. But I put most of the weight on my own shoulders. It is my responsibility to deliver. I don't have behavioral problems, so most of the kids do the work. Most of my kids believe they can do the work. But I have one kid who all he can do is put his name on the paper. Some kids make excuses. I talk to them to find out what their needs are. I adjust to what they can do. For example, in science I will do an oral assessment rather than a written one for some of my labeled kids. A couple are so unmotivated. I seek out other resources.

And educators even altered how they assigned students to teachers, all in the name of making sure that students encountered the adults best suited to work with them:

We try to match teachers with the personalities of the students. There are only two or three real difficult students. The bigger picture is to not label the kids and to help bring up their self-esteem. The big, big picture is to connect with kids. We should not make their lives miserable.

The bottom line, according to one teacher, was simply this:

These young people can't afford to have any more adults give up on them. We must stay committed to their needs.

Parents aimed most of their written survey comments at issues that they believed teachers were not handling constructively. One of their primary peeves was that too few schools engaged in the sort of needs recognition and accommodation process described above. Parents recognized that teachers were in an excellent position to know what students' needs were and to take the instructional, and personal, steps necessary to incorporating these needs into an effective way of working with each student. It frustrated them endlessly when educators did not do this. Three succinctly conveyed their feelings:

Teachers are in the capacity to see firsthand who is being raised or who is raising themselves. They should intercede and give a hug, smile, or handshake or whatever works and take off the blinders [that make them think] "ain't my child, ain't my problem."

Some of the teachers [at the high school level] take a "my way or the highway" approach.

The teacher is not teaching my child at his level and has no intention of accommodating my child's needs.

Parents' assessments about the number of teachers who willingly shouldered the responsibility for student success themselves agreed with the results of our teacher interviews. We found that only two of the 15 schools we studied in the two districts had enough such teachers to warrant our considering "It's my job" to be a shared, schoolwide belief. For example, one teacher described Granite Junior High, profiled in Chapter 5, in this way:

With respect to student work, it is not "if," but "when." The whole staff believes that.

In the remaining schools, we located no more than a handful in each who shared such a commitment.

In large part, this scarcity apparently was a function of the difficulty of implementation. Taking an approach that assigned the responsibility for learning to teachers required them to be incessantly vigilant. By asserting that all students could do the work they were given and that it was the teacher's responsibility to ensure success, teachers found that they had to hold students accountable *and* not let them off the hook when work was due. They had to be unwavering "nags":

> Kids need to be trained to be responsible. If kids don't turn in their homework in my class, what happens? I keep on them. I keep them after school. I believe that being lenient breeds laziness.

> [With students who do not do their work], we bring them in front of the team. We make sure we use their peers in cooperative learning situations. We look for outside help. They are not allowed just to sit and be an in-school dropout. We also make our expectations very clear. Kids know how to work here. It is always very obvious when a new student transfers in from another building. They don't know how to work.

This was tough work, according to the teachers. They said it would have been much easier to abdicate their responsibility to the ever-handy scapegoats of student motivation and home environment. However, this segment of educators resolutely refused to succumb to such reasoning, as the following two teachers illustrate:

> It's my fault, not theirs, when they are not successful. I need to be more in tune with what motivates them.

> We are their way to success, their door or path to a better world, regardless of what's going on in their personal lives. We just need to pull them through, allow them to see that they can be better.

A third and fourth teacher provided the labels that we eventually attached to this way of thinking about working with students who traditionally did poorly in school:

> I am definitely a *"No excuses"* teacher. For example, take one boy in my class. He is very bright, but there is something in the

house that keeps him from doing his work. If someone has to expect more, it has got to be me. The effort has to be sparked. After
all, he is only 8. Instead of being negative and saying he is hard-
headed, I try to be more positive. I insist that he will do this.

My job is to give curriculum and instruction no matter what
their shortcomings. [If they aren't motivated], I take it as a failure
on my part. There is something that should reach them, one tech-
nique; there's some way to reach everyone. There is a way to
reach them, and *it's my job* to find it so that they can succeed.

These two labels—"No excuses" and "It's my job"—capture the
essence of what the teachers in this section said. Their students had
countless problems, ones that many children should not have to face,
and yet none of these sufficed as a reason why teachers could not work
with the students and make them successful. "No excuses" therefore
meant that there were no explanations for a student's lack of satisfactory performance in school that a teacher should use as justifying his
or her inability to nudge, prod, or nurture the student to demonstrating
the desired level of work. "It's my job" reflected teachers' acceptance
of their obligation to make such an effort with every student. Thus the
two labels interchangeably denoted that student success was ultimately
the teachers' responsibility.

Teachers such as these did not claim to be quixotic idealists, hope-
lessly tilting at the windmills of educating poor children. Indeed, had
they had to work in heroic solitude, they argued, they would eventually have failed. Thus we heard a noticeable hint in their comments
that their success at making students successful in large part hinged on
working in concert with others in the building, a point that Chapters 5
and 6 illustrate in detail:

Each school building must act as a loving family unit. We solve
problems as a building team. We are accountable to ourselves
and team members. Each part is important for the success of the
building. Students know they can't divide us. We are strong as a
whole unit.

I have changed my philosophy a bit. I believe it is our job [the
school's job]. I make more use of other resources—the principal
and the resource room teacher. I have learned that you need the
support of everyone. While I know it is my job, I realize I need
to use the resources of the entire school. It is our problem, not

the kids', if they are not motivated. We have to make kids have a reason for coming to school. Also, I am willing to help even at the sixth-grade level, not just my 27 students.

I see it as a team effort involving downtown, building administration, parents, and teachers all being on the same page with expectations and having everyone involved.

Such attitudes were not the norm throughout the two districts, although this is not to say that we found the majority of teachers to be unmindful of students' plights. In fact, many of them had intentionally committed themselves to working in low-income situations. They eventually, however, found that certain obstacles were insurmountable. They mentioned two repeatedly: student motivation and family situations. These two issues filtered into many of the educators' qualifications to the "All can succeed" mantra. We next look at each qualifier in turn.

ALL CHILDREN CAN SUCCEED . . . IF THEY ARE WILLING TO TRY

Some of the teachers who claimed that students were not holding up their end of the learning bargain were adamant that students needed to take most of the responsibility for correcting the situation. At some point, these teachers reasoned, students would be expected to motivate themselves, either in the "real world" or certainly in high school. Thus "hand-holding" would be counterproductive if it went on too long. A teacher explained at some length:

> Are you familiar with the expression you can either give a man a fish or you can teach him how to fish? I try to teach them responsibility and that they will succeed because they want to. My job is to teach science, social studies, etc. My job stops at 3:00. It is their responsibility from 3:00 P.M. until 8:30 the next morning. For example, today I threw some homework in the trash that had no names on them. I have been telling them all year long that they need to put their name on it. Eventually they have to accept consequences for their actions. It won't click if I keep holding their hands and allowing them to put their names on after they have turned it in. I finally drew the line and told them they would get a zero for today's homework assignment. I do that because I want them to worry (i.e., take responsibility for them-

selves). It is my job to pass on information, but it is their job to do homework. There is only so much I can do. I can't knock on the door of their home and ask if they are reading. My job is to set clear consequences for their actions. Not all kids are conscientious about their work so we have to show them that if they don't do it, then they won't succeed.

Such teachers did not come across as callous to us. They seemed sincere in wanting students to succeed, and they clearly were willing to help students. It was just that they desired some reciprocity for the effort they were making. As a result, some teachers required students to try first before they would step in to help, as in the first instance below, while others started out offering assistance but withdrew it if the child did not respond, as in the second case:

Kids have to want to try. I have one child in particular who always has to have someone helping him. I keep monitoring his progress. If he tries, I will help. If not, I just keep walking.

You can help all kids, but some choose not to [work]. We have a repeat seventh-grader this year. His prime goal is to not do the work. I just can't spend all of my time continuing to help him when he doesn't respond. I help all of them at the beginning of the year. But after four marking periods, I have beat myself up. We need to put some more responsibility on their shoulders. If you don't, they think they can get away without doing the work.

Teachers argued that it seemed fruitless to continue to harp on students to complete their work when they saw such a large number of young people who were detached and uninterested in school:

I have students who deliberately disengage themselves by putting their heads down or choosing to talk to their friends instead of listening to instructions. They give up before they begin, have an "I can't attitude," and don't want help.

The teachers regarded this behavior as a student's conscious choice:

Although many are disinterested, lazy, and don't do homework, they are capable. They chose not to learn.

And the teachers began to resent the implications of such student behavior for what happened instructionally in the classroom:

> Recently there is a decline in students—few fast learners, less abilities, and lazy. I must change my teaching style. I water down vocabulary. The teacher must become a parent. I resent having to spend all of that time at it. It's not my responsibility.

This teacher appeared to be on the way to giving up on students. But the reader needs to remember that all the teachers (and parents) from whom we are quoting first acknowledged that all students could succeed in school. So we are not drawing from the population of people who had already decided that this ideal was not at least theoretically possible.

As mentioned above, most teachers in this group tended to see student success as a matter of balanced responsibility, a two-way street where both the teacher and the student had to reciprocate one another's efforts:

> Learning needs a stimulus and a response. Does the kid want to learn? They [students] need to use their memory. It [education] is totally interactive. Too many parents feel it is the teacher's job only. The kid is a key factor. For example, I have a girl who comes from a single-parent family. The central ingredient [to her success] is motivation. She came in today with two pages of notes on Clinton's state-of-the-nation address. I had asked them to watch it but didn't suggest that they had to take notes. That is in comparison to other students who didn't even bother to watch.

Clearly teachers were not saying that learning and classroom success were completely up to the students. Instead, unlike the "It's my job"–type comments from the first group of teachers, these educators identified a point at which their responsibility ended. Thus, as the teacher below explained, teachers still had to assess students' learning needs and come up with a way to address these, but not unconditionally:

> I recognize there are learning-style differences. I make an effort to meet those different needs, but the kid needs to want to do it. It is not a one-way street.

In some ways, however, there was almost a tautological element to what teachers said. If students worked hard, then teachers would make sure that they succeeded. That is, teachers would not give up on students who had not given up themselves:

I believe that working hard brings success. But it has to be the same with the kids. If a kid is not willing, you can work hard but nothing will happen. I refuse to accept the responsibility if the kids don't work hard and are not conscientious. I don't fail kids who work hard. But I will fail nonworkers. I was the other way when I first started teaching, but I learned that kids have to bring something to the table. I gave a C to a student this year who failed every test but who did the homework and came after school for extra help. I won't give up on kids willing to work forever. That's what I am here for.

Teachers justified this reasoning by arguing that as students grew older, it was incumbent upon both students and teachers to develop the students' ability to take responsibility for their actions. For the teachers who were among those described in the first section of this chapter, this burden did not lift from their shoulders until a student had actually demonstrated such an ability. For the teachers who qualified their belief in student success with the proviso that students had to try, the shift in responsibility seemed more chronologically determined, usually by the time the student reached high school—although the following teacher obviously felt that middle school teachers had to promote a little anticipatory socialization:

As an eighth-grade teacher, I would be remiss if I didn't put the responsibility on students since students have to make decisions and take responsibility for them. They have to learn to live with the consequences. For example, with grading of papers, they have to learn to take the consequences if they don't turn in the work. I can't keep giving them extensions and allowing excuses for not doing work. We have to guide them, but eventually they have to make decisions for themselves.

These teachers thus believed that students needed to accept more responsibility for their learning. They asserted that teachers had to assist that process, but that it really was their duty to step back at some point:

I believe it is the kids' responsibility, but I will do everything to help. But the final outcome is with the kid—it's their life. I tell them the only person you hurt if you fail is yourself. I am always here to offer them ways to succeed.

> I think it is mostly the student's responsibility, but I need to adapt lessons to the kids' learning styles. If they don't take responsibility, they will go into the real world without realizing that they never have someone standing over them.

Still, several of the teachers almost contradicted themselves. They were committed to working with low-income students, and therefore they still looked on their students' success with pride. When they recounted favorite stories of students who had overcome the odds to do well later in school or in life, they often acknowledged that the students probably did so because teachers somewhere along the line did not give up on them:

> I believe you need to put more on their shoulders. We have some students, no matter what I do, who aren't motivated. They don't see that graduating from high school is any big deal. But then I see them 5 years later, and they have turned out fine. Someone pushed them.

It was this sort of thinking that put this group of teachers into a quandary. They really seemed to be sympathetic with the notion that the responsibility for learning was theirs, but they could not bring themselves to adopt that position unequivocally. Instead, they sat on the fence. They worried about the detrimental effects of "spoon-feeding" students, but they also worried whether the teachers' contact with these students would be the students' last opportunity to taste success. A concluding string of quotes reflects the almost agonizing tone the teachers injected into their comments:

> I struggle with this on a daily basis. I not only give as a teacher but also as a surrogate mom. I worry whether I should spoon-feed them or just give them enough support. I guess I am kinda like a rubber band being pulled from one to the other, and I feel the tension going both ways. I think it is important to see what the individual student needs. Those may vary from day to day and from subject to subject. I do believe that we have to wean them before they move on to the high school. I try and treat them as individuals and ask what they need now: more support or have the apron strings cut.

> I never give them a task where they can fail without having the right tools. That is especially true with my kids. I give them the

tools, but it is up to them to pick up the tools. I don't walk them through each step. I will stop if it seems they don't understand the tools. If I do [steps] one, two, and three with them [a lot], they will expect me to do it every time.

I give them direction and I must put the first foot forward, but the next step is theirs. You have to be supportive, but if you do all the work for them, you do them a disservice. Kids have to fail to learn.

It is my job to help them. But I sit on the fence as to my belief. I lean to the child being more accountable, but I feel a big responsibility is for me to help them.

I take all the responsibility. I make them do their best work. But I am not with them 24 hours a day. They need to take ownership of their work. I make sure they do. Basically, I am in the middle. Even though I give them homework and I will stay after school to help them or come in early to work with them, they still have to take some responsibility. It's like the old saying, "You can lead a horse to water but you can't make him drink."

I am of both mindsets. Kids need the tools to do it. They need to have a belief in their own ability. But they must also say "yes" [to the invitation], even with help after school. I don't give up, but eventually the student must take the responsibility. They are part of the community, and they must play a role. Some kids don't know how to do that. If they don't take the responsibility, they will be getting into society and will fail. We need to move beyond teaching them knowledge, we must also work with them on learning responsibility. We can't make them learn, but we can motivate them to want to. If they fail, it's because they choose to.

ALL CHILDREN CAN SUCCEED . . . BUT SOME DON'T BECAUSE OF THEIR FAMILIES

It was difficult for some teachers to put the blame for failing to complete work on students, particularly on the younger children. So these teachers argued that the main reason they were not more successful with all students was the inadequacy of the support system available to children and adolescents. In most cases, those failings resided in the home.

Some teachers perceived a decided lack of discipline in the homes. They felt that students' misbehavior outside school was met with impunity. Otherwise, young people would not act out so much inside school:

> I believe we need to make the parents have a part in their child's behavior, have parents come in to baby-sit or send their children home. After a few times of the parents being inconvenienced, the children's behavior may change. Children should not be allowed to continuously disrupt me doing my job for students who are trying to learn.

For the majority of teachers, however, the source of students' behavior had to do with parents' not placing enough importance on learning as a core value, as the following two teachers argued:

> Some kids seem to be as limited or as good as their homes.

> It would be helpful if the parents felt it [schoolwork] was more important. There needs to be more parent involvement. None of my parents showed up at back-to-school night. The district needs to get "downtown parents" more involved. It's like it is all up to us [the teachers].

And even if students' enthusiasm in the early years did not reflect a lack of emphasis on education, eventually the "home" effect would show up:

> Even without parental intervention, some of our students do want to succeed and enjoy learning, but the older they get and the more difficult the work is, the harder it is to keep them in school when the parents are not interested. They learn excuses from them, and if they aren't expected to succeed, they often quit trying.

Teachers who took this perspective, like those in the previous section, claimed that they strove to counteract the considerable obstacles they faced as instructors in low-income communities but that they often reached a point where there just was not much more they could do:

They [fellow teachers] need parents to support them. For example, I had two students who were leaning the wrong way. I went out on a limb to help them, but eventually I had to turn the responsibility over. Ultimately, if parents can't help, I hit a wall. I try everything, e.g., I will keep them after school to help them, but I can't go home with them.

Consequently, teachers with this mindset gazed upon colleagues who accepted no excuses as unrealistic:

We can beat ourselves over the head, but we can't do it all. Kids succeed at different rates. I don't see the motivation and support at home for all to succeed. There are just so many things a teacher can't control. Having a "No excuse" classroom is a nice "up-here" goal, but I don't see it as happening.

Parents, in their written extensions to survey responses, agreed with the teachers about the need for a strong family influence. A few phrased it positively, as something they needed to do or were already doing:

It is our job to guarantee our children becoming successful citizens.

[My child likes school a lot] because her parental upbringing has taught her the importance of education and has shown her that learning can be fun.

The majority of parents' comments, however, sounded very similar to those of teachers. They focused on what they saw as lacking on the part of other parents:

I feel if the parents would get more involved in what their children do in school and help them in any way that they can, it would help that child have a better attitude about school . . . and a good attitude is what counts.

And, echoing the teachers again, parents described the eventual classroom effects of poor discipline at home:

[My daughter] would like it "great" if the teachers did not have to be doing so much parenting and disciplining to other students. The parenting is not getting done at home anymore, and it's not fair to the teachers. The teachers are doing the jobs the parents should be doing at home when they could be doing the job they're getting paid for: to teach! Parents are not spending enough time with their kids at home helping with their homework and encouraging them.

IMPLICATIONS OF THE VARIED MEANINGS OF "ALL CHILDREN CAN SUCCEED"

It is not hard to imagine the consequences of qualifying "All children can succeed." Qualifiers set limits. They specify the conditions under which a particular goal or activity is likely to succeed. "All children can succeed . . . if they make an effort to do so." "All children can succeed . . . if their parents play an active role in their education." "All children can succeed . . . if teachers supply all of the encouragement and support necessary to ensure that success."

Each of these qualifiers was undoubtedly "true" for the individuals who advocated them. Certainly they were born of experience and therefore represented a person's best assessment of what was possible to achieve in educating poor children. However, there was a critical difference among the qualifiers. The first two required someone else to do something before educators could succeed with their responsibilities. "If a student doesn't want to learn, I can't make him (or her)." "If those parents don't care about education, their kids won't either." Students and parents had to make changes first.

The last qualifier, however, looked inward—to teachers and administrators. Those adhering to this idea essentially argued that they could not alter the conditions outside school that impinged on student performance; they could only affect that which was under their control. Thus the external conditions could not serve as valid reasons for student failure.

We do not want to portray one set of beliefs as valuable and good and the other two as worthless and bad. Indeed, the above quotes, particularly in the section on student responsibility, revealed a dilemma that was clearly troubling for many people. But we do think that they have different implications for closing the gap in achievement between low-performing and high-performing students.

Matters of home versus school are, of course, endemic to debates about the roots of the problems in educating low-income students. For us to simply assert that this debate can be put to rest by telling educators not to worry about that which they cannot control would do little to advance the cause of improving schools in poor communities. Thus the apparent short shrift that we gave to the parents and students' home situations above, at least in terms of the relative length of the three sections, did not reflect our sense of the topic's importance. Instead, we reserve much more room to discuss parents' and teachers' thoughts about each other's roles in the next chapter.

3

Parents' and Teachers' Beliefs About Each Other's Role in Educating Students

Educators frequently said to us that low-income families rarely involved themselves in their children's education. They backed this impression with comments about having seen only a handful of parents and guardians at school and inferred that this absence reflected a lack of interest. Because so many of the educators we talked to claimed that their low-income students could succeed in school if adults at home would become more actively involved, we decided to take a closer look at both teachers' and parents' assumptions about each other's educational role.

We were especially interested in this issue because recent research suggests that inferences about parental presence at school and commitment to education might be more myth than reality. For example, in a study of 12 poor families, Nieto (1996) discovered high involvement at home—but in ways that were not visible to educators. She found that parents constantly stressed the importance of going to school and going to college and that children looked at them as positive role models, not so much because of their educational achievement but rather because of their strength and resilience in coping with difficult circumstances. The children felt that they could exhibit these same qualities by staying in school and following an avenue that, for a variety of reasons, had been unavailable to the adults. Nieto observed that although poor parents did not directly help with homework often, they actively monitored it by asking about its content and encouraging its completion. These families also promoted native-language use and adherence to cultural values as means of promoting academic success. Thus, rather than being an impediment to students' education, these families felt that they were reinforcing and enforcing high educational expectations for the children.

In this chapter we present reinforcement for the idea that low-income parents valued education but demonstrated this in ways that teachers might not have seen. We begin by carefully looking at teachers' dim views of parental involvement and then counter these with parents' survey responses concerning their—and teachers'—beliefs about education. Following this discussion we detail the ways that parents engaged children about school and present these adults' opinions about the support the schools gave them. Our conclusion is that, in ships-passing-in-the-night fashion, each group believed firmly that it cared more about education than the other did.

TEACHERS' PERSPECTIVES ABOUT NONINVOLVED PARENTS

In the previous chapter, we noted that most staff members in the two districts had internalized the belief "All children can succeed" but that a sizable number of them felt that families impeded classroom success. Even clearly dedicated teachers who excited and motivated students to learn saw distinct limits to what they could do with children academically. In our interviews with them and their open-ended responses on surveys, teachers elaborated four different interpretations of how parents hindered educators' efforts.

Parents Had More Opportunities to Influence Children

Some teachers felt that what happened at home often dwarfed teachers' ministrations and prevented students from making substantial effort in the classroom. Parents simply had more opportunities to influence students than did teachers, and teachers perceived that this influence was not positive. One reason for this, three teachers claimed, was a matter of time:

> I think that without support from home, children who could achieve will not be as successful as they could be. I can make a difference but I am fighting an uphill battle. Students are with me 6 hours a day but at home 18. It's difficult to overcome all they see and hear at home.

> I have them for only a few hours a day. The students come from and return to the same home environment. There is zero accountability on the part of parents and children. It's very difficult to combat that.

I'm an idealist, so I would like to believe that my teaching has an impact on all of my students. I hope they will expect from themselves what I expect of them. However, I am also a realist and I recognize the fact that 7 hours a day cannot compete with the 5 years before they start school and the other 17 hours a day they spend out of school.

Embedded in these comments was the assumption that what happened at home ran counter to what teachers were trying to do in school. The phrases "all they see and hear at home," "the same home environment," and not being able to "compete" with time spent out of school juxtaposed teachers' values and actions with those of parents. It was unclear on what basis teachers were making these judgments. Indeed, none spoke of making actual home visits. Nevertheless, they seemed to think that parents' increased opportunities to influence their children automatically would negate teachers' schoolday efforts.

Parents Were Disrespectful of Educational Values

Against this backdrop of perceived negative influence, teachers pointed their fingers at specific parental behaviors that they inferred were reflections of a lack of interest in academics and a disrespect for school norms. For example, failure to follow up on teachers' attempts to reach them meant that parents did not care enough to do so:

> Parents don't respond to phone calls or progress reports. These children have been passed through the system, and I can't catch them up to speed.

Other explanations were possible. Practically speaking, some parents may not have received certain messages; culturally speaking, some parents may have felt it was inappropriate to speak directly with school officials. But the teachers believed the actions, or lack of them, to be direct evidence of parental lack of interest.

Likewise, preschool children's misbehavior when parents did come to school was taken to be indicative of this same lack of caring, despite the fact that any parent with young children frequently holds his or her breath when making a public appearance with them:

> It's simply not true that stimulating lessons that are well planned and encourage students to strive for high standards is a solution to all the educational problems. Parents and students are being

rude, disruptive in school. You should see the moms allowing preschoolers to run and scream through the halls of school while classes are in session, and it is becoming more and more acceptable. Teaching manners, morals, consideration of others, would help greatly.

Even a teacher's attempt to explain parents' behavior implied a sense that domestic troubles common to many households (job stress, divorce, drug or alcohol abuse, etc.) somehow and invariably had negative educational implications in low-income families:

> No matter how much parental contact with parents I make, their [students'] caregivers often don't care. They are so overwhelmed with their own problems that their children's seem trivial.

Certainly, it could be the case that teachers' actual experiences with their students' parents were the basis for the above observations. In fact, one teacher who had grown up in impoverished but educationally supportive circumstances was also unable to see similar care in today's parents:

> I put full blame on the parents' shoulders; they don't care nearly enough. Having come from a background of extreme poverty, I attribute much of my success to very supportive, though uneducated, parents who cared deeply about my school progress.

Regardless of the accuracy of teachers' perceptions, a widespread belief in low-income parents' devaluing of education prevailed.

Parents' Negative Attitudes Reflected Their Own School Experiences

Teachers felt that more than likely these parental attitudes were carry-overs from the parents' schooldays. They hypothesized that the low number of high school graduates and college attendees in the adult population was primarily a function of an unwillingness to stay in school. This lack of success, then, established an ambivalence toward education in the home that turned students away from the fun and significance of learning:

> Unfortunately, all parents do not value education or perhaps had a miserable school experience for whatever reason. These attitudes color how they interact with their children and their children's

school. Therefore, some students may not value their education as strongly as I would like.

In other words, parents still carried baggage with them from the days when they were in school and were unable to rid themselves of those feelings when meeting with people in the same roles with which they had had unpleasant encounters:

> Some families seem to see school as the enemy, too, so the children don't have as positive an outlook on education.

Parents Were Unwilling to Work with Teachers

Finally, teachers talked of the need for a team approach to educating children—the whole-village idea. They complained that school leaders and, indeed, society expected much too much of teachers and held them accountable for results over which they had little control. This frustrated teachers greatly, even more so when they perceived that they had reached out to parents for their help and been repeatedly rebuffed:

> Teachers are only one aspect of a child's life. I feel over the years too much responsibility has been put on the school. We are being asked to raise many children without help from the family. They are shrugging their responsibility and asking many times for the school to do it all. *Together* [emphasis in original survey response] we make a difference. The school needs to note this also—that a teacher cannot always make a child successful.

> In certain instances, teachers can certainly "make a difference" and inspire almost anyone. However, without proper support from home, a stable family life, etc., it would be an "uphill" battle. The public school alone cannot provide the necessary tools for great achievers and cultivated individuals.

Taken together, the above four interpretations of how parents affected student success reinforced the teachers' belief that they rowed upstream alone. At best, they felt, parents exerted a neutral influence on children and at worst a detrimental one. Teachers, therefore, portrayed themselves as being more committed to students' academic success than parents were. Interestingly, as we will see in the next section, parents felt the same way—only the roles were reversed.

PARENTS' VIEWS ABOUT TEACHERS

There were undoubtedly parents who were not as supportive of their children as teachers would have liked. However, parents had the same concern about teachers. In fact, survey responses show that parents believed strongly that they were more committed to education than teachers.

We asked parents to weigh in on a number of educational issues relevant to their communities. Since both districts had involved parents in strategic planning sessions that we attended, we had access to discussions that helped to frame survey questions about important education-related beliefs—ones that both directly implicated students and that eventually made their way into district mission statements. Overall, 974 parents responded to the survey, indicating how strongly they felt about each issue as well as how strongly they thought teachers' felt about the same issue. Parents used a 5-point scale that ranged from Strongly Disagree (1) to Strongly Agree (5).

Table 3.1 reports an overall mean score for all parents completing the survey for each belief statement and a comparable mean score generated by these same parents for the strength of teachers' beliefs. There was a statistically significant difference between the two means for all statements.

In a nutshell, parents said that they felt more strongly than teachers about *all* 15 belief statements. Whether the statement concerned the role of the school, student differences, teachers' commitment, or matters of pedagogy, parents indicated that they appreciated the values implicit in the statement significantly more than teachers. Of course, their perspective was biased and mostly uninformed by conversation with teachers about these specific issues. But then, so were teachers' opinions formed in isolation from parents. The interesting point is that, in the admitted absence of much interaction, parents mistrusted teachers' concerns for their children's educational needs just as teachers mistrusted parents'.

We looked more closely at whether parents with different backgrounds felt differently about the strength of their own and teachers' beliefs. We compared parents (1) whose children were in elementary, middle, and senior high school; (2) who had a high school diploma or less, who had some college credits, and who had graduated from college with at least a bachelor's degree; and (3) who reported their child (children) as being a top student, a good student, or an average to poor student. We would have preferred to have also collected information on family income, but district administrators deemed that information

Table 3.1. Mean Scores of Parents' Beliefs and Parents' Views of Teacher Beliefs

Belief Statement	Parents' Beliefs	Parents' Views of Teachers' Beliefs
Teachers should encourage students to remain in school.	4.66	4.31
All students have special skills and talents. The job of schools is to identify them and promote their development.	4.55	3.76
A significant role for the school is to enhance students' views of themselves as learners and as worthwhile people.	4.52	3.92
Classroom content and activities should be designed to permit all students the opportunity to acquire knowledge at higher levels of understanding.	4.47	3.89
Student mistakes should be used as opportunities for further learning.	4.45	3.84
Schools should provide opportunities for teachers to create more caring environments (i.e., communicating to students a sense of future) in their classrooms.	4.43	3.74
How hard a student works contributes to how successful he/she will become.	4.41	4.22
Schools should promote the view that every child can learn challenging content and achieve at high levels if given quality instruction.	4.34	3.84
Classroom content and activities should incorporate out-of-school experiences that have meaning to students.	4.32	3.68
School grades should reflect a combination of academic performance and effort.	4.30	4.02
School administrators should ask for input from diverse parent groups.	4.29	3.61
It is important for teachers to view students as having talents in areas that are often unrecognized.	4.28	3.58
Student motivation to learn is enhanced by introducing schoolwork that is relevant to students' lives.	4.20	3.60
The pace at which a student learns should not be a factor in influencing the opportunities for that student to learn.	4.19	3.51
Student grouping practices place students in situations where learning expectations and opportunities are limited.	3.21	3.01

Notes: All questions used a 5-point scale ranging from Strongly Disagree (1) to Strongly Agree (5). $N = 974$. Difference between means was statistically significant for all statements ($p < .05$).

too sensitive and worried that such a question would greatly reduce our response rate. Instead, we used parent education as a proxy for socioeconomic background and found that overall 28% of the parents had a high school diploma or less, 33% had earned some postsecondary credits, and 37% had a college degree.

Parents' statements about the strength of their beliefs were not affected at all by the level of school (elementary versus middle versus high school) in which their child was enrolled. The same was also true for parental education and student success, with the exception of a few beliefs where parents with more education and more successful children reported stronger commitment than did parents with less education and less successful children. The main finding, though, was that strength of belief was not statistically associated with either school level, parent education, or the academic success of their children.

Parents' views of teachers' beliefs were also not affected statistically by either parents' education level or the academic success of their children. In other words, parents at all education levels and all levels of children's performance reported that teachers did not uphold these beliefs as strongly as they did. The one area where there were differences was with school level. Parents of elementary school children reported that teachers felt more strongly about the beliefs than did parents of children in secondary school for 13 of the 15 survey items.

So, who was right? Were teachers correct in criticizing parents' lack of interest in education, or were parents accurate in claiming they felt more strongly about educational issues than teachers? We were able to address this issue with three survey items that were common to both the parent and teacher surveys. These findings are summarized in Table 3.2. We found that parents had stronger positive feelings about all three beliefs than did the teachers.

PARENT AND SCHOOL ACTIONS
IN SUPPORT OF STUDENT LEARNING

If parents perceived themselves to be so supportive of education, why did educators persist with their negative impressions of parental involvement? One hypothesis was that teachers inferred parental attitudes from student behavior in school. If students acted like they did not value education, then their parents must be acting in that way as well.

Teachers, of course, did not have ready access to data that would

Table 3.2. Mean Scores of Parents' and Teachers' Beliefs on Three Items Common to Both Surveys

Belief Statement	*Parents' Beliefs*	*Teachers' Beliefs*	*Parents' View of Teachers' Belief*
	(N = 974)	*(N = 1,357)*	*(N = 974)*
All students have special skills and talents. The job of schools is to identify them and promote their development.	4.55	4.33	3.76
The pace at which a student learns should not be a factor in influencing the opportunities for that student to learn.	4.19	3.89	3.51
Student grouping practices place students in situations where learning expectations and opportunities are limited.	3.21	2.72	3.01

Note: All questions used a 5-point scale ranging from Strongly Disagree (1) to Strongly Agree (5).

bear on this circumstantially based inference. Thus another hypothesis about parents was that their actions were often invisible to teachers. This latter point was reinforced by the second part of our survey, which investigated how parents involved themselves in their children's learning and how schools attempted to involve parents.

We asked parents to report on the frequency with which they engaged in activities supportive of their children's education. We organized the survey questions around a set of six standards that had recently been adopted by the National Parent–Teacher Association and endorsed by 30 national education organizations, including teacher and administrator professional associations. Based on the work of Joyce Epstein (1995), the standards included the categories of (1) communicating, (2) volunteering in the school, (3) student learning at home, (4) school decisionmaking and advocacy, (5) parenting, and (6) collaborating with the community.

Because involvement was a two-way street of parent involvement and school solicitation of that involvement, we designed measures for the six standards that addressed how involved parents were and how well they thought the schools reached out to them. To assess each standard category, we created a single composite score based on a combination of several survey items. (The interested reader is referred to the Appendix for a complete description of the items and a definition of each standard.)

Table 3.3 summarizes the results of these analyses across the six standard categories, with the categories displayed in order from most to least parental engagement.

Perhaps the most striking finding was the differentiated nature of the roles that parents saw themselves playing. That is, parents reported (despite teacher comments to the contrary) that they were very actively engaged in parenting activities and activities associated with learning

Table 3.3. Mean Scores of Parent Engagement and School Support for Six National Parent–Teacher Association Standards

Standard	Parent Engagement	School Support
Parenting	4.66	2.74
Learning at home	3.98	2.93
Communicating	3.77	3.40
Community collaboration	3.71	2.78
Decisionmaking and advocacy	1.62	3.35
Volunteering in the school	1.43	2.92

Notes: Each parent engagement standard is a composite of survey items ranging from Never (1) to Very Often (5); these scores are self-assessments of parental engagement. Each school support standard is a composite of survey items ranging from Does Very Poorly (1) to Does Extremely Well (5); these scores are parents' assessments of schools' supportiveness. $N = 974$.

at home. In marked contrast to their heavy involvement in these two areas, parents said that they were not at all engaged in decision making and advocacy or volunteering in the school. The difference in mean scores between the categories of active engagement and those of low engagement was remarkable—a difference of 3 points on a scale with a maximum difference of 4 points.

Parents reported being most heavily involved in the two sets of activities that were most removed from the school setting and least involved in two that required an active presence in the school. Thus teachers' complaints that parents were not actively involved in their children's education were understandable but inaccurate.

A comparison of scores between parent involvement and school support involvement invited some interesting speculation. For example, what parents said they did *most* frequently was what the school provided the *least* support for—parenting. Likewise, what they said the school did best (communicating) was an area in which parents were only moderately engaged. Thus there apparently was a mismatch between what parents and educators were looking for in each other, a mismatch—bred of ignorance about one another's intentions and actions—that led to counterproductive finger-pointing.

On closer examination, however, we found that parental engagement and school support were higher at the elementary than the secondary level, that parents with greater levels of education reported more engagement, and that parents with more successful children were more actively involved and thought their schools to be more supportive of their efforts. These findings lent partial support to educators' assumptions about low-income parental involvement but did not necessarily challenge Nieto's (1996) argument that these parents' actions tend to be "behind the scenes."

But there was a message that went beyond the numbers detailed above. Parents did not see the schools, and the teachers in them, as being as supportive or as committed as parents would have liked them to be. The final section of this chapter presents several recommendations parents had for the schools about promoting more involvement.

PARENTS' RECOMMENDATIONS TO TEACHERS

We solicited parents' written comments on the surveys about what would help their children to be more successful learners. More than half of the survey respondents availed themselves of that opportunity. Below we draw only on parents who had less than a college education, since teachers had singled out such parents for criticism. These parents' comments provided an additional rebuttal to educators who place the blame for student failure on families.

Parents saw the value of *extra help* for their children and called for teachers to devise multiple means of providing it. Some parents issued a general plea for teachers to devote more time to students who needed it:

> There should be additional help for the children who have shown a need and a desire for it!

> Teachers at the junior high need to make themselves available for the students, they [teachers] tell the parents at the conferences that they will meet with their child but when the child/student comes to that teacher, they are too busy.

Other parents wanted the provision of extra help to be less informal:

> There should be a place that we can send students in the summertime to help the ones that are slower during the schoolyear and let them catch up instead of eliminating schoolwork out of the [usual] summer [calendar].

Parents' ultimate goal in their comments seemed to be to make sure that teachers did not give up on students and made sure that students worked until they got "it":

> Some teachers try to give too much information at once and expect a child to retain all of the facts with very little time before moving on to something else.

> Don't ever give up. If they [students] do bad on a test, give them another chance to repeat the test in a day or so for improvement.

There was a general concern among parents that teachers and the curricula they taught were not demanding enough for students and that *consistently high expectations* needed to be implemented throughout a school to produce top-quality results:

> The school system as a whole should raise the level of expectation a notch higher. I do not wish to see staying at a level or lowering the level just so that the kids can have "self-esteem." In the

long run, such false "self-esteem" does not serve them in the real world.

Parents were also very explicit about their need for *enhanced lines of communication*. For parents, there never seemed to be enough:

> Teachers need to make the effort to make some phone calls to the parents to offer one-on-one discussion about a student, especially if teachers or parents see potential. I know of some teachers who do take the time to tell the students and the parents. I would love to see it done with all, regardless of if it is academics, sports, arts, and politics.

While parents wanted to know more about the events in school and to be kept abreast of homework assignments, the biggest concern seemed to be with not having adequate information about their children's progress in the classroom. The harshest complaints came from parents who said they did not find out about academic problems until they saw them on a report card, which they argued was too late a time to intervene:

> Teachers should not wait so long to contact parents when their child is doing poorly in class. They shouldn't wait until the student has already lost that credit.

Parents were adamant that teachers needed to offer more *variety in the instructional day*, with an emphasis on active learning. They were especially critical of teachers who relied only on traditional lecture formats:

> They need to realize that all children are not textbook materials [learners] and that some kids do very well in many other things.

But parents were also quick to point out that good teaching required more than unrelenting monitoring and motivating pedagogy. Indeed, they made special note of the need for *quality relationships* between students and teachers. The most common word parents used to illustrate what they meant by quality relationships was the call for teachers who *cared*:

> The teachers do not take enough interest in our kids.

My child does better one-on-one in an after-school program.
We need more caring teachers.

High school teachers don't care. [They put] all responsibility on the students.

CONCLUSIONS

Parents believed strongly in a set of values that would promote their children's success in school while reporting that teachers did not grasp those values so strongly. Moreover, parents reported high rates of engagement on some activities associated with student learning but very low rates on others, and they were only moderately pleased with the level of welcoming support they were obtaining from the schools. While we had no direct measures of parental income that would enable us to claim irrefutably that both the lower- and higher-income parents held these views, we were able to determine that the perspective was consistent across self-reported levels of parent education and student success. These proxies, combined with the sizable survey sample, convinced us that low-income adults were at least somewhat suffering from an undeserved reputation.

Moreover, somehow teachers and parents had both formed negative opinions about each other while claiming that they themselves served as major positive and compensating forces in children's educational lives. The ironic point was that while they were complaining about one another, both ignored the power of forming an alliance, of building on this unrecognized but mutual commitment to enabling students to succeed in school.

We did not see that teachers who adopted the "No excuses" or "It's my job" philosophy looked at parents in any more positive light than the other teachers. All we know from our data is that the former regarded parental involvement as a welcome but not necessarily expected development whereas the latter used its absence to establish the limits of their effectiveness.

4

Taking Responsibility for Effort and Excellence in the Classroom

Chapter 2 described a group of teachers who felt that they were responsible for ensuring student success. They talked an impressive game—perhaps one that was too difficult to actually carry out daily in the classroom, at least according to two other groups of their peers who stated that lack of student effort and minimal family support limited teachers' effectiveness. To shed more light on how practical a "No excuses" philosophy was, this chapter provides four examples from three different school levels of what teachers who proclaimed that "It's my job" to make all children successful looked like in real life.

The teachers we write about—Edna Sanders, Craig Smith, Margaret Waters, and Jim Evans (all pseudonyms)—differed from one another with respect to race and gender (an African American female, a Caucasian male, a Caucasian female, and another Caucasian male, respectively) and experience (a year from retirement, midcareer, early career, and second year, once again respectively). All four taught in the same school district, with most of Edna's and Jim's elementary students moving on to Craig's junior high and then to Margaret's high school. The secondary schools, however, were more diverse racially and socioeconomically because students from several neighborhood schools filtered into them. The elementary students whom Edna and Jim taught in their self-contained classrooms were nearly all low-income and African American.

The four of them had different personalities as well as varied teaching styles. Edna was vibrant, almost evangelical in her delivery; Margaret was quietly steadfast in keeping each student's attention on matters of writing and literature. Craig was an entertainer, with the "audience" in his hand and the front of the science lab his stage; Jim earnestly worked one-on-one, yet always kept a watchful eye on everyone else.

What the teachers had in common was a belief in their responsibility for student learning. Each espoused the notion that it was his or her job to make sure that all of the students succeeded in school, regardless of the students' motivation and support at home. However, we did not choose to devote a chapter to them because of what they said. That decision was based on what they said, what they did, and what students said they did. All three pieces of information—an interview, an observation, and students' comments—had to complement one another before we were willing to consider the teachers as exemplary of the "It's my job"/"No excuses" philosophy.

None of the teachers reflected the norm in their respective schools; indeed, according to students, they represented an extremely small minority of their respective faculties. Perhaps that is why these adults stood out so clearly in the students' thoughts about being successful in school.

Once again, the image of what success meant to teachers can be raised as an issue. Did the teachers demand only effort, or both effort and excellence? As is the case throughout this book, we highlight only teachers and schools that combined the two. Lipman (1998) convincingly describes the limited benefits for students who have traditionally done poorly in school when educators define success solely in terms of good behavior. The following teachers recognized this pitfall and committed themselves to making their students academically competitive. This commitment came alive when we watched them in the classroom and when students talked to us about them.

The sections below present excerpts from our field observation notes (these are italicized) and transcripts of teachers' and students' oral statements and exchanges. For the most part, we limit our commentary in Chapters 4 through 6, preferring that study participants speak for themselves. Chapter 7 serves as a "conclusion" to all three chapters and draws on the descriptions to elaborate and extend what we see as the meaning and value of teachers' refusal to set limits on what they can accomplish with students who traditionally have done poorly in school. A reader impatient for our interpretations of the "data" might want to flip back and forth between whichever of the next three chapters is being read and Chapter 7.

EDNA SANDERS: SIXTH-GRADE SELF-CONTAINED

Edna's school served mostly minority students. All but two of the students in her sixth-grade class were African American. Traditionally, the students in the school performed poorly on the various standardized tests the district administered. The school, in fact, was the lowest-performing elementary school in the district.

As will be seen, students toed the line for Edna, but it is important to point out from the outset that the classroom was not completely without problems. All the adults we spoke to in the building acknowledged that the student population posed behavioral challenges, to put it mildly. By no means did Edna have an atypical class. In fact, in this classroom, as in the others observed in this particular building, students—sometimes quietly and sometimes loudly—"ragged" on other students. Teasing was constant, if not merciless. While such behavior was minimal during our observation, one of the interviewed students reported that it still happened at times and that she was often unable to ignore it:

> INTERVIEWER: Are you learning a lot?
> STUDENT: Yes . . . not really. Every time we start something, someone act up and we got to start over. It cuts out our learning time.
> INTERVIEWER: Are you a good student?
> STUDENT: I don't know. (*She starts laughing.*) I can't; there are so many people with bad influences. If I tried, they would call you a "goody-goody."
> INTERVIEWER: Why?
> STUDENT: If you get good grades.
> INTERVIEWER: Why?
> STUDENT: 'Cause they can't. They want you to be like them. They can't be like you.
> INTERVIEWER: Could they?
> STUDENT: They could if they tried.
> INTERVIEWER: Why don't they?
> STUDENT: Because they wanna be the leader.

Another student also noted the disruptive behavior of other students. However, she reported that she could not resist joining in at times:

> INTERVIEWER: Do students behave?
> STUDENT: Some people act up, like mostly the boys . . . they just nasty sometimes.
> INTERVIEWER: Does that distract you from your work?
> STUDENT: Sometimes it's distracting, sometimes it funny. But it ain't supposed to be. Yesterday I was in the same group as [another student] and I started laughing.
> INTERVIEWER: Is there anything the teacher can do?

> STUDENT: It always gonna happen.
> INTERVIEWER: Is that a problem?
> STUDENT: If I try, I can ignore it.

And another—a male student—downplayed the boisterousness even more:

> It happens every once in a while, but when they get wild, they get unhyper, and chill. We be good like most of the time. Like if the teacher go out, [the teacher will] say "be quiet" and tell people to take names.

Finally, another female student described ways of getting around this distraction from other students:

> INTERVIEWER: Do the students prevent you from working?
> STUDENT: Sometimes they do. If I have a lot of work to do, they wouldn't. But if you get done, they will distract you. I ignore them. When I'm done, maybe I talk.

This discussion of students' classroom behavior is not intended to diminish the value of Edna's approach to teaching these students. Instead, it provides a realistic description of conditions that often cause teachers to decide that some students just do not want to learn and, therefore, that it is okay for them to fail. Edna, however, resisted this reasoning and felt that such a situation made it even more urgent to find ways to keep instruction and student learning as the primary foci. In an inimitable rapid-fire delivery, Edna had this to say about whether all children can succeed in school:

> I told the parents "I believe every child can learn; you make sure your child wants to learn." I tell them, "Your child should be able to say I learned some new thing or more about something I already knew; if the child says 'no,' come see me 'cause something is wrong." We don't have any kids who cannot do it. They have been allowed to get away with it. I believe they will perform well if they know I am concerned about what they do. I do think we have a group that someone has given up on. It is real easy to not expect much. That bothers me. We've given them an excuse to not do well. One of my major things is the kid might be LD [learning disabled] or severely handicapped but in here, "we" is all of us. If you can't do it, I will make allowances. You

will do 25 problems [the full assignment], but you may need more help to do it. Kids aren't the problem; adults are the ones finding the excuses.

In the classroom, Edna made sure that there was no room to find excuses for poor performance. Through a mix of strategies—allowing no grade lower than a C (students had to redo assignments until they attained this grade), monitoring each child's work daily, connecting classroom lessons to students' everyday experiences, enabling students to work with one another, and providing as much help to each student as was necessary for the student to learn—Edna cajoled, teased, berated, and praised the students on their way to improved achievement.

In the lesson we observed, the class reviewed a social studies test from the previous day. Edna explained that the students tended to do poorly on standardized reading comprehension tests, and so the lesson would use the text material and the test to help her and the children understand how they had arrived at their answers. One of the students described the lesson like this:

INTERVIEWER: What were you learning about today?
STUDENT: Social studies.
INTERVIEWER: What were you doing?
STUDENT: We do over the test. Some people scored poorly, and the teacher wanted to know where people got their answers from; they messed up.

Thus the lesson was to emphasize how the students came up with their responses as much as what the answer was.

Edna had established a grading policy that no student could get less than a C. However, she emphatically pointed out that she did not *give* every student a C; instead, Edna did not allow any student to *earn* less than a C. She explained:

My policy is less than a C must be done over. Usually there are 90% who correct their answers. I tell the parents, "Anything your child does can be done over."

The students we interviewed clearly were aware of the distinction between receiving a grade and earning one. This understanding came through even though they had different perspectives on the policy. One student had incorporated the policy into her definition of what a good teacher is:

INTERVIEWER: What's a good teacher?
STUDENT: To do what supposed to.
INTERVIEWER: What do you mean?
STUDENT: To make sure all kids get the work done. If they don't get good grades, let 'em do it over. Like our teacher.
INTERVIEWER: What does your teacher do?
STUDENT: Ms. Sanders is different.
INTERVIEWER: How?
STUDENT: Ms. Sanders more strict.
INTERVIEWER: What do you mean by "strict"?
STUDENT: Like, uh, Ms. Sanders wants you to get your work done. If you don't, you stay until you get it done.
INTERVIEWER: What if you don't stay?
STUDENT: If you do that, you get sent home; and when you come back, you still got to do it.
INTERVIEWER: Do you like that?
STUDENT: I like it.
INTERVIEWER: Why?
STUDENT: 'Cause I want to pass and not get stuck in this grade another year, or I'll be driving to class. Ms. Sanders say, "You gonna be driving your family with you to school."

A second student, a male, interpreted this policy in a benign way—that is, rather than viewing this "nothing less than a C" requirement as a mandate, he saw it as a "second chance":

INTERVIEWER: Why did you say your teacher is nice?
STUDENT: Ms. Sanders don't be like we gotta have our homework in. If we get a D or E, Ms. Sanders *let* [emphasis added] us do it over.
INTERVIEWER: Do you like getting to do it over?
STUDENT: I likes it.
INTERVIEWER: Why?
STUDENT: 'Cause Ms. Sanders fair 'cause she give ample time to get it done. Some students think Ms. Sanders is being mean. But if you can't get it, Ms. Sanders give you another chance.

This same student also understood that this second chance did not excuse the student from responsibility for achieving. Instead, it put the responsibility for passing directly on the student. As he explained it:

STUDENT: Ms. Sanders never let people settle for D or E; Ms. Sanders don't let people get away with it.
INTERVIEWER: What kind of teacher do you prefer?

STUDENT: Like that. Ms. Sanders give us a education. Other teachers don't care what you do. They pass you to be passing. Here, I pass my own self.

Another student, a female, seemed a little more hesitant to laud Edna's toughness, but she nevertheless was resigned to having to achieve at a certain level. She discussed Edna's approach with an interesting mix of comparative praise and personal resentment:

STUDENT: Ms. Sanders different from other teachers because she not gonna sit there and let you do what you wanna do; you do what she said. In other classes, the teacher didn't care; they let us sit there.
INTERVIEWER: So what do you have to do to be a good student in the Ms. Sanders's class?
STUDENT: You have to do your best. You can't say you can't do it. Ms. Sanders not gonna take it. You gotta try and get A, B, or C. If you get E, she want you to do it over. She said, "In junior high you might not have the chance."
INTERVIEWER: Do you get mad if you have to do it over?
STUDENT: Well, it depends. I don't like getting Es; I settle for Cs. She not very pleased with it, and my mom wouldn't let me settle with an E. When I get E, at least I have a chance to do it over. But when Ms. Sanders tell me to, I say "I ain't, I ain't gonna do it."

Edna fought students with this attitude tooth and nail each day. During each lesson, including the one we observed, she was determined to find out whether and what every single student who was present was learning. This led Edna to develop a strategy for monitoring their performance each day:

My style is I want to hear them respond so I know they're getting it. If you don't talk, I don't know what's going on. From day 1, you're expected to respond. The worst thing is to go through school and no one knows what you looked like.

In the lesson, Edna therefore constantly asked students, all students, to indicate whether they knew the answer to a question. Sometimes this meant that Edna waited until every student had raised his or her hand, and sometimes Edna went around to each of the tables and checked with each student. Either way students could not make it through a class without indicating what they knew. Typical of such monitoring were the following two requests:

> That would be nice [i.e., the answer that students were calling out loud] . . . if everybody was answering! I didn't hear you. Again! All read the answer!

> (*speaking to the whole class*) Where do you find the answer? Put your finger on it so I know you got it. (*Edna walks around and looks at each child's finger.*)

Sometimes Edna's making sure that everyone knew the right answer involved proving that everyone was wrong:

> *The teacher raises her voice asking for the answer, and more and more students raise their hands, several stretching high and others waving their arms.*

> How many looked on page 2, in paragraph 2, to get the answer? Raise your hand high!

> *A student near me whispers to the group that they are wrong. [The answer is not at that location on the page.] But the teacher is yelling now for the students to show that they had found the answer in that location and so they all keep their hands up, even the student who is arguing that the answer is not there.*

> I'm looking to see who knows! You're ready? Ready? Everyone? . . . WRONG!

> *The students moan that Edna has lured them into the trap.*

> Look at the top of the page. There's the answer. So it looks like I get company after school after all [referring to a promised penalty—in jest—for the students' being wrong].

Students picked up on the message that the only way Edna could know whether they were learning was for them to speak out—either in public or in private:

> Ms. Sanders give you another chance, so you can get the problems. Sometimes it be hard to do the problem. She say if nobody ask, she guess you know how to do it.

One student reported a downside to Edna's constant checking. Not surprisingly, this was the same student who had expressed some resentment over having to do everything over to get a C:

> INTERVIEWER: What makes a class boring?
> STUDENT: When the teacher say the same thing over and over. I'm like, "I heard you the first time."
> INTERVIEWER: Why does the teacher say it over?
> STUDENT: Because a lot of people are slow.
> INTERVIEWER: But is what you are learning important?
> STUDENT: It's important; but some of it be boring though. But I know it is the stuff we need to be prepared for the next grade.

Edna argued that students' understanding of a lesson was directly related to whether students had had experiences in real life that could be connected to the lesson:

> The kids think subjects are isolated. In their minds, there are things that click, but you have to bring it to their minds. They've had enough experiences outside school, and seen enough TV, so things are familiar to them; but they can't make the connections. They can't remember they saw it. So we have to do that in the class.

A couple of examples of how Edna attempted to put this belief into action arose during the observation. In both, Edna was trying to get the students to think about or imagine what living in Brazil would be like. In the first example, Edna tried to get the students to list the kinds of experiences they could have that would give them at least an idea of what Brazilian culture is like:

> What kind of experience would help you understand this selection?
>
> *The students make a list: "attend a political conference," "host a foreign exchange student," "eat their foods," "go to visit a South American."*
>
> Why? You said, "Yes, it would help." Now, tell me why.

In the second, Edna took an aspect of living in Rio de Janeiro and got the students to draw an analogy to situations with which they were familiar:

TEACHER: If you are in a squatters' settlement, are we rich or
   poor?
STUDENTS: (*Various answers are called out.*)
TEACHER: I don't think we're sure. Pull out the dictionaries. Did
   you find it?
STUDENT: It ain't in here.
TEACHER: What?
STUDENT: (*The same student repeats.*) It's not in here.
TEACHER: I could have sworn I heard you say "ain't."
STUDENTS: (*Students finally find the word in the dictionary and
   several read the definition.*) "People who settle on land that
   is not necessarily theirs."
TEACHER: Think about it. In big cities, what group of people now
   are kind of like squatters? They settle on land that is not nec-
   essarily theirs.
STUDENT: Homeless people.
TEACHER: Not because they want to. Now where do they live?
STUDENTS: (*Several students call out.*) On the street. Under a
   bridge.
TEACHER: So this gives you an idea about how squatters live.

Edna, in the interview, explained what she was trying to do:

In every lesson, there are some questions only the good kids are
gonna get. But it's designed so that every kid can be right everyday. This is important because when they do give a wrong answer some time, they don't feel bad. They know the lesson will
evolve and everyone will get a chance.

Thus, she said, tying classroom content to students' everyday experiences kept the students engaged in the lesson, through recognizing
that they had some insight or information to offer. At the same time,
Edna believed that this foundation of success fostered students' aware-
ness that it was all right to make mistakes or not to understand some
point being discussed in class. Students seemed to have picked up on
this:

INTERVIEWER: What do you do when something in class is difficult to understand?
STUDENT: I raise my hand, or go to the teacher and ask. But I
   don't blurt it out.
INTERVIEWER: Do you mean that people are embarrassed to ask?

STUDENT: No, people in our classroom are not embarrassed.

INTERVIEWER: Why?

STUDENT: Everybody like to try and my teacher say "that is not funny" when somebody ask a question.

And from another student:

Everybody going to make a mistake. I like doing work on the board 'cause if I forget how to do it, she come over and show it to me. If people laugh, at least I can say I'm trying.

Groups played an important role in Edna's classroom. Students sat in them all the time, and clearly the teacher wanted students to learn to rely on one another as resources and to have opportunities to try out ideas and answers. In the interview, Edna explained that it took at least half of the schoolyear for the groups to finally begin working in a way she found acceptable. By that time, Edna expected the groups to become an invaluable resource for students. Edna frequently admonished students during the lesson to take advantage of this aid. Three different examples follow, among a host of them that could have been chosen:

You're not working as a group if you are not talking right now!

Now what is a fact? A fact can be proven. Not a fact is an opinion. Now which of these sentences is a fact? One of those is a fact. Raise your hand if you find it. If you are sitting in a group [which they all are], help each other. If one person in a group has a hand up [showing that the student knew the answer], all should have it up. Every hand up? Great! What is the sentence? (*They all say it.*)

Raise your hand high if you know the answer. If you can't find it, you will stay after school. You are sitting in a group. (*They all start talking to one another.*) (*Reacting to the increased noise associated with trying to find out the answer, the teacher jokes.*) I feel bad you guys feel like you don't want to stay with me after school.

According to two of the students, the groups seemed to exhibit the supportive characteristics that Edna desired:

INTERVIEWER: How do you like to work: in a group or by your-
   self?
STUDENT: In a group, 'cause if everybody pitch in, we all get the
   right answer.
INTERVIEWER: Does everybody pitch in or does one person do it?
STUDENT: In my group, everybody do the work.
INTERVIEWER: Do you work in groups a lot?
STUDENT: A few times we went in rows, but most of the time we
   can all get more done in groups; we help people.
INTERVIEWER: How do you get more done?
STUDENT: With groups, you communicate with everybody.
INTERVIEWER: But what if you don't get along?
STUDENT: My teacher move 'em. Ms. Sanders have, like, a thing:
   You can't have cousins in the same group or friends or peo-
   ple will talk. My teacher says she gonna put it [the class] in
   one big group if we do that.

There was a danger, however, in some students' becoming overly reli-
ant on others in their group and allowing the others to do all the work.
As one student noted:

> Some things I like to do by myself so I can concentrate, instead
> of telling others in the group, so they can find the answer. Some
> people expect someone else to find the answer.

Edna made sure that students knew that she was concerned about
whether they were learning and that she would help them in whatever
ways possible, even in ways that the students themselves might not
welcome. Edna elaborated on this strategy:

> I have some say, "I don't want a C." Then we stay after school. I
> say, "I can stay all night." I enforce it on Friday when the build-
> ing empties out fast, and we are the only ones left here. I also
> make house calls and show up on the porch with a book in my
> hand. My key phrase is, "I'm like one of your family." I just
> don't accept mediocrity. The world is too demanding, too com-
> petitive. The kids need to think they are doing better each day
> . . . to say I did the best I could at the end of the day.

In other research we are doing, students dwell on the importance
of a teacher's communicating that he or she is willing to give students
all the help they need (Wilson & Corbett, 2001). The students in this
study were no different:

INTERVIEWER: What is a good teacher?
STUDENT: Like when you need help, Ms. Sanders don't give up. She help you work it out.
INTERVIEWER: Why do you like that?
STUDENT: Because if I don't get help, then I don't wanna do it.

But this same student complained that this support was not necessarily received happily:

INTERVIEWER: What is your teacher like?
STUDENT: My teacher just stricter, so many rules.
INTERVIEWER: Do you prefer teachers that are strict?
STUDENT: I prefer strict, but sometimes it gets on my nerves, especially when my teacher is talking to me.
INTERVIEWER: What does your teacher do?
STUDENT: Ms. Sanders always call my grandma.
INTERVIEWER: What does your grandma say?
STUDENT: She say I know better.
INTERVIEWER: Do you?
STUDENT: Yep.
INTERVIEWER: So your teacher and your grandma are right?
STUDENT: Mm-hmm.

Nevertheless, receiving such help was an important determinant of whether students stuck to doing a task or not. Agreeing with the above student's earlier comment, another student stated:

INTERVIEWER: What do you do when something is difficult?
STUDENT: I get frustrated.
INTERVIEWER: Then what do you do?
STUDENT: Somebody ask me a question and I get snappy 'cause I don't understand it.
INTERVIEWER: Do you give up?
STUDENT: I ask the teacher how you do the question and Ms. Sanders explain it to me, and then I find the answer.
INTERVIEWER: Is not knowing how to do something a reason why other students sometimes give up?
STUDENT: They don't know how to do it, so they don't. If you don't know how to do it, all you gotta do is ask and she help you.
INTERVIEWER: Why is it important to not give up?

STUDENT: You got to put your mind to it, you gotta focus, 'cause in the future you got to know it.

Especially when dealing with adolescents, help often was not limited to just the academic variety:

INTERVIEWER: Do you feel that teachers understand students?
STUDENT: Yeah, I do. When I was having problems in my household, my teacher try and help me out. I have a bad attitude. Ms. Sanders helping me, she understands.
INTERVIEWER: When does your teacher listen?
STUDENT: In the hallway or after school.

As indicated above, students were cognizant of what Edna was trying to accomplish, and they reported that the desired effects were in fact being achieved:

INTERVIEWER: Are you learning a lot in this class?
STUDENT: Yes.
INTERVIEWER: Is what you are learning important?
STUDENT: It's important. Definitely. Later on if you have kids in your life, your kids might need some help. I don't like to be embarrassed to tell my kids I don't know how.

Or as another student claimed:

INTERVIEWER: How do you like school?
STUDENT: Good.
INTERVIEWER: Why?
STUDENT: 'Cause when I come every morning I learn, and Ms. Sanders teach me what I need to know, and Ms. Sanders give me help when and if I need it.

CRAIG SMITH: JUNIOR HIGH SCIENCE

I walk into this junior high classroom just after the science lesson has started. It is a small class of only 11 students. The students are seated on stools in groups of four around tall lab tables. This is clearly a hands-on lab with plenty of work in progress scattered throughout the room. As the class is finishing up the warm-up activity from the chalkboard, the teacher is ener-

getically taking care of three or four tasks simultaneously. He is taking the roll, noting to anyone who will listen that "about half of the class is absent; does anyone know why?" There is silence from the students. He also is reminding students that they have a heredity lab due. His comment made to me in an earlier conversation—"You can't give up"—comes to mind.

I battle it out to the end. You can't give up. You always gotta try. I've had days where I dismiss a kid basically. But, overall, no, I don't do that. I've got a short memory. The next day I forgive and forget. I got kids who say I'm always on them. Part of it is the level here. They're going through a lot of changes. Everybody eventually will say, "I can do this." I try to make that realization come sooner rather than later.

In his gentle but firm way, he has just let the class know that he will not let them off the hook. On another twist to that same theme, in the very next breath, he says that he was surprised no one came to see him for help yesterday after school. He jokingly comments, "I guess everyone knows the work."

Craig walked a tightrope. He strove to be consistent and insistent in his demand that each student do all the work and to remain flexible enough to use different means of reaching them. Finding a balance between using alternative ways to engage students in classroom activities without also completely individualizing his overall expectations for students was clearly a challenge:

We don't do a lot of reading out loud because of the kids' level. We do "buddy reading." I have to be aware of the students having weaknesses. So I do lots of explanations. I use multiple intelligences that says there are lots of other ways for people to learn. I do demonstrations, hands-on. But I worry how will they be better readers if they don't read.

The real testament to the success of Craig's recognition of the need for multiple ways to reach students was in students' acknowledgments of the value of his actions for them, as the comments of two of his students demonstrate:

INTERVIEWER: What does Mr. Smith do if you are confused and don't understand?

STUDENT: He stops everything and explains it. He keeps trying something different until you understand it. He doesn't leave you on your own. You don't learn nothing like that!

STUDENT: He tries to include everybody. Like, if you are not paying attention, you know he is going to call on you. But he won't embarrass you. If you can't answer him, he will ask it in a different way.

INTERVIEWER: Are other teachers like that, too?

STUDENT: No, they're different.

INTERVIEWER: How are they different?

STUDENT: They are not as active as he is in helping you learn. If he sees the class is moving slow or people are having a hard time, he holds off the test or he does more labs. He does that a lot. He also gives us extra work. Other teachers don't do that. He wants to do so many different things so kids will learn.

Students respected, and apparently desired, Craig's refusal to give up on them. His tenacity came through repeatedly in class. An incident at the very end of a class period was an excellent illustration of that. Rather than just giving the students an assignment and escorting them out the door, Craig carefully crafted an encounter that tested not only whether the one targeted student understood the work but also whether the whole class was following along. Here is how he did it:

The class has just finished reading a section from the textbook on gene mutation that has been punctuated with discussion and animated explanation of examples by Craig about what is meant by the fairly dry text. The class is getting ready to do an experiment where they will cross one hybrid albino corn plant with a pure-bred albino corn plant and will observe what effect having white leaves will have on the corn plant. He passes out a lab sheet, which, just by its title—"Attack of the Mutant Corn Seed Lab"—introduces some levity and humor. He starts reviewing the problems he wants them to do: "Make a data table for homework to record how all the plants grow for at least 10 days after they first sprout; remember that you will have data for two different kinds of plants. We have done data displays before, but for those of you who are totally stumped about how to organize the information, I have placed a sample display on the back of the door."

Craig then goes on to show them how deep he wants the seeds planted, how to make holes with their fingers, and the two different conditions for planting (individual pots versus a big fish tank of soil). Just before the bell rings, he stops the class and turns to an Hispanic male student and asks him if he knows what he is doing for homework—pausing to wait for a reply to make sure that everyone hears the answer and that he can check to make sure it is right. He also asks the student where he can go for a sample if he is stuck. The student points to the classroom door. Rather than just telling the class again what the homework is, he uses the student as a checkpoint to make sure his initial instructions were understood, doing it in a way that ensures the rest of the class was also listening.

When students exited the door after class, however, the chances were good that the finished period would not be their last instructional encounter with Craig. To be truthful, it seemed that he hounded students to seek him out at free moments, especially after school. Students in his class were quick to point out that this was an important component of his teaching style—providing "extra help" opportunities:

INTERVIEWER: What does your teacher do if you don't understand?

STUDENT: He gives us examples. He always has examples. Like today, everyone needed an example [of the data chart]. He also has us come in after school.

INTERVIEWER: What does he do with the after-school time?

STUDENT: He puts it in a way so everyone understands. He puts it in a different way—so that we are both laughing and learning.

INTERVIEWER: What else does he do?

STUDENT: He give us extra work to do. Others [teachers] don't do that. He wants to do so many different things so that kids learn.

INTERVIEWER: How often do you come in?

STUDENT: Once or twice a week.

INTERVIEWER: What do you do?

STUDENT: He takes 5 or 10 minutes to go over what was in the book and he shows us how to do it. He gives us extra credit if we come in. Also, if you make the honor roll or the respect code, he will buy us lunch at Burger King.

"Not giving up" on students did not stop with using a variety of strategies, continually checking for understanding, and offering extra help after school. Craig also kept very close tabs on their progress and always let them know where they stood in terms of being successful in class. Students also highly valued this trait:

> STUDENT: He keeps on us a lot. We have assignment sheets we have to do. He checks that every day. He adds up all the points and gives us extra points when we bring things in signed by our parents.
>
> INTERVIEWER: How do you know where you stand?
>
> STUDENT: He has three places you can go to check up on yourself: You can go to the grade book, there is a chart on the wall, and he has us keep track of our progress in our own books. There ain't no other teacher who keeps up with you like that. He gives you extra credit any time you want.
>
> INTERVIEWER: What if you fail to turn in an assignment?
>
> STUDENT: He will give you a zero, but he will let you make it up by doing a report on current events. With other teachers, only they keep your grades [in their books] and you don't hear no more about it.

Another student similarly described Craig's close attention to work completion:

> INTERVIEWER: How do you know where you stand in his class?
>
> STUDENT: Every week or two he will call us up and tell us. He is always telling us to make up missing work. We can do current events to get extra credit.
>
> INTERVIEWER: Why does he do that?
>
> STUDENT: He wants us to do a good job. He just doesn't give up on us. He wants us to do the work.
>
> INTERVIEWER: Do you prefer that kind of teacher?
>
> STUDENT: Yeah.
>
> INTERVIEWER: Why?
>
> STUDENT: He is more flexible and keeps explaining things. He doesn't leave you on your own. You don't learn nothing like that. My math teacher—he explains it one way and then gives us the rest of the period to do it. [Mr. Smith] stays on top of you all the time. He has us carry an assignment sheet that we keep in a folder. It helps us keep track of the work we are missing.

As Craig explained:

> When they really keep track of their own grade, they tend to do better across the board.

A student concurred that this strategy of making sure students knew what they needed to do as well as how to do the work was ultimately an effective one:

> INTERVIEWER: What does your science teacher do that helps you learn?
> STUDENT: He gives us examples and explains it more than other teachers. He helps us understand and he makes sure we understand.
> INTERVIEWER: How does he do that?
> STUDENT: He gives a different definition, and then he acts it out for us.
> INTERVIEWER: Does that work for you?
> STUDENT: Yeah, it gets in your head and it stays there. He makes sure we all know it. He doesn't just say "Here's the assignment." He makes sure everyone knows what is going on and gives us time to understand.

Prodded, Craig admitted that it would be easier to just let students slip by without doing the work and justifiable if one felt that students should shoulder most of the responsibility for motivating themselves to work. The long-term consequence, however, would be that a portion of the students would never experience much success in school:

> CRAIG: If I would let some put their heads down, some would.
> INTERVIEWER: Do you let them?
> CRAIG: No, this is the time of year I'm fed up with it. I try to get them motivated, get them to experience success, get them to feel good about themselves. That's the biggest reason I do it.

The above suggested that Craig looked at possible discipline issues from an instructional point of view. That is, rather than looking at a student's putting his or her head down on a desk as a violation of a class rule, he thought of its implications for learning. This was illustrated clearly by a very brief incident in which a student entered the classroom in the middle of the discussion about gene mutations, almost 15 minutes into the lesson. The tardy student had no slip from the office indicating why he was late, nor did Craig elect to interrupt the lesson and demand an explanation. Rather than disrupting the flow of the class, Craig simply announced to the student what page in the book they were working on and quickly got on with the discussion, without missing a beat. For his part, the student quickly settled into the task.

Later, in a conversation in which he ruminated about his classroom management practices, he offered this explanation:

> I tell 'em I'm just a big eighth-grader. We have a good relationship. I'm in their "quality world," as they say. The ones I'm having to slow down with look at it as I'm always on them.

The relational aspect of Craig's association with students was significant to him. Craig suggested that he tried not to miss any opportunity to challenge students to think about the value of an education. He said he knew from the high school's statistics that many of these students were not obvious candidates for graduation, absent some intervention. That spurred him to become obsessive about reminding students of the consequences of any short-term decision that portended the prospect of not finishing school. Craig explained his approach in these terms:

> I talk about things like college, careers, like working at McDonald's as opposed to a corporation or to being an engineer. I question when it is possible for a 16-year-old to drop out. I tell them some doors will be closed. I give more direct motivation and say "you're gonna fail [if you leave]." I try to get a hold of the parents. Little successes let them know they can do it. I want them to move from more extrinsic motivation.

Craig appeared to take a genuine interest in students' well-being beyond the classroom, often taking the time to help them work through personal and social problems. One student, in fact, liked most that he was willing to hold "heart-to-heart" conversations with the class:

> STUDENT: Sometimes he will just stop what we are doing and have a heart-to-heart talk.
> INTERVIEWER: Can you give me an example?
> STUDENT: Yeah, we have a student in the class, [name], who shot himself. Mr. Smith took the time to help us work through this.

At the heart of what made students successful in Craig's class when they had not been successful elsewhere was how he made science interesting. Not all content was intrinsically engaging to the students; indeed, they said, most of what they learned in school was not. Craig then manipulated the situation to draw in the students. He used thought-provoking rather than recall questions, interjected humor and games, incorporated students' strengths into what they were asked to do, and recast content in real-life situations.

Here is a brief snapshot of how that strategy played out. Before visiting that scene, however, let us preface the vignette with a student's comment about the value of Craig's applying the content to situations that had meaning for students and doing so in a way that interjected some levity into the classroom:

> He teaches us the lesson but he also jokes at the same time. He is more exciting, and I pay attention more. There are not too many who fall asleep in his class.

Craig's eighth-grade class is reading from the science textbook about gene mutation. The content is technical and not very exciting, the kind of stuff that quickly tunes out students, especially those who struggle with challenging content. Craig's goal is to get the class to take notes on the key concepts, but rather than just having them write notes off the board or dictated by him, he stops after each paragraph and carries on a little dialogue, translating what has just been read into something that has more meaning for the students. The class has just read a paragraph in the book that discusses whether mutations are a good thing or not. Craig begins by posing a question.

CRAIG: When you hear about mutations, what do most people think of?
STUDENT: Bad things!
CRAIG: If I said I wanted to give you a mutation, what would you think?
ANOTHER STUDENT: I wouldn't want it.
CRAIG: Most mutations are not helpful, but sometimes one can be.

He then asks for another student to read the next paragraph in the textbook, which provides a definition for mutation. *He tries to get students to construct their own definition.*

CRAIG: Can someone take a stab at giving me a definition?
STUDENT: It is a change in the chromosomes.

Several students start writing in their notebooks.

CRAIG: That's a good start, but I don't want you to write just yet. When scientists manipulated things in the lab, did they get what they expected? No. A mutation produces something unusual. It is unexpected and unpredicted. Can someone give me the old college try at a revised definition that is more than just a change?

STUDENT: It is an unexpected and unpredictable change.

CRAIG: Good! Everyone should write that down. Did you get that down? [a question directed to a particular student]

STUDENT: No.

So Craig pauses and waits until that student also gets it written down. After Craig is sure that everyone has the definition written in their notebooks, the class then returns to the textbook, where the next passage deals with how mutant genes get passed along. Again, there is some more technical language in the text about transmittal requiring sex cells. Craig stops and asks them to return to their notebooks.

CRAIG: I want you to put a dash after your definition and write in your book "it must occur in a sex cell to be passed on to the next generation." (*Craig walks up to look at a student's notebook.*) What have you got?

STUDENT: I am not sure.

CRAIG: (*to another student*) Why don't you help [the first student] out?

Craig pauses briefly, as if debating about whether to just push on with the content or to stop and offer an illustration that might better make the point come home for the students. He opts for the latter.

CRAIG: Now, let's suppose you went to the dentist. You remember how they always drape you with a big lead-lined apron before they take x-rays. Let's suppose you had a very careless technician who failed to put the apron on you and kept taking x-rays because he messed up each image and in the process the overdose of x-rays altered some of your genes. Could you pass that on to your children? (*There are some affirmative and negative nods.*) To change your genes it must affect your sex cells, not just your body cells like the x-ray did.

STUDENT: Is it 100% sure you will pass along a defect?

CRAIG: That is a great question!

Craig proceeds to explain the probability of such an occurrence.

The class returns to the textbook but not before several other student questions. A student then proceeds to read the next paragraph, which offers additional detail about whether a mutation is good, bad, or neutral.

CRAIG: Is a mutation good, bad, or neutral?

Following several shouted answers, Craig gives his own humorous example, which he illustrates by jumping up on the lab table so that he is now towering over the class. The students look up to him as if this is normal behavior, but also with complete attention. While this seems unusual to me, I can see in the students' faces that this is pretty standard fare and they seem to be enjoying it. At a minimum, he has gotten all their attention.

Let's assume I inherited a gene that made me 9 feet tall. Let's put that into perspective. Who is the tallest player in the NBA and how tall is he?

A student suggests Shawn Bradley and volunteers that he is 7 feet, 6 inches tall.

Well, imagine me at 9 feet and I have to bend down to pat him on the head. But for this to continue, you need to keep reproducing that gene. If that happened to a 9-foot player, then eventually it might change the nature of the game. Let's assume I had another defect that generated six fingers on a hand. Would that be helpful? I guess it might be if you were a typist.

Craig finally summarizes the point he wants to make after offering several more examples. He tells the class that there are three kinds of mutational effects and he asks them to write them in their notebooks: "99.99% of mutations are harmful. Some are neutral. Very few mutations are helpful." The students copy this into their notebooks.

Recounting this episode was not intended to suggest that every teacher has to jump up on a table and imitate a 9-foot basketball player, but rather that this teacher took fairly dry text and embellished it with examples that had meaning in the students' lives. And a potentially boring lesson became etched in students' consciousness.

MARGARET WATERS: HIGH SCHOOL ENGLISH

The "angry and annoyed voice" of a female high school English student:

Who did you think you are? Why don't you just leave him alone? You're the one who gave him up; you can't just came back when he finds someone else. You smile and gloat like you know he's yours. That's not what he's telling me. Don't act all innocent. I've heard all those stories about you. You're not what you seem. You make me sick. The way you hang all over him and laugh at all his jokes. You know how I feel about him, and you still do all this right in from of me. If you're trying to make me jealous, it's working. You've proven your point, you can stop now. You wear your little skirts and all your prissy little clothes. You think you look so cute. You're just a little hoochy. You've got your mental problems, too. He doesn't want to get involved with all that. Just leave him alone.

Her translation of that voice into the Shakespearean tradition:

Who doest thou thinkest thou art? Why doest not thou leave him to himself? Thou denied him, do not return once he hath found another. You smirk with confidence. Nay, he speaks not of thou to me. Thou imagine thyself to be chaste. Word has been spake to me otherwise. Thou art a mockery. Thou maketh me ill by thy acts of foolishness which art like a harlot. Thou knowest of mine affinity and still yet thou provoke him in my presence. Thou yearns to maketh me vengeful and thou succeeds. Hath thou stated thine affection? Thou clothing and spirits are of a wretch and thou mind is light.

What goeth on here? Attracting students to English literature is one of the perennial challenges of the American high school. A worthy battle in and of itself, but Margaret Waters—an English teacher in a large high school serving a roughly 50–50 minority–majority student population—viewed this challenge as only a minor part of a larger issue. The issue was what to do with students who traditionally fell through the cracks in the floors of high school classrooms:

> Some students are driven, even if their parents are not, but students without parents as professional models are less likely to see a future.

So Margaret worried often about how to hook students into learning, particularly those who seemed so detached from learning. One solution was connecting classroom content to students' lives:

> I believe in the student-directed classroom. Curriculum must be related to their own lives. They must be given the opportunity to make choices and participate in meaningful activities. When we studied *Julius Caesar*, the students could elect to portray meaning through art, a play, or a paper. For *Othello*, I asked them to write about a time when they were jealous or translate a passage from Shakespeare into Ebonics. Kids can prove they've understood in different ways. I need to know what motivates and interests them.

Margaret did not feel that any one idea would work with all the students. Indeed, any of her lessons were likely to reveal her using a variety of strategies. For example, the lesson that resulted in the Shakespearean translations similar to the above used (1) individual work (writing in a jealous and "mad" voice) and sharing those initial statements with a partner to generate interest in the day's activities; (2) a teacher-led instructional time in which students examined speeches in a Shakespearean play, paying close attention to language that they did not understand; (3) a return to individual work to rewrite their passages as Shakespeare might have; and (4) a final opportunity to share these passages with the class.

Even the mundane was worthy of creativity. In a previous lesson, the class was going to use a study guide to review the material in a chapter of the literature book. Adhering to her belief in the value of a student-directed classroom, Margaret decided the students should identify the critical questions to answer about the chapter—and in small groups so that all would have to contribute. Moreover, the products of these discussions were not lists but rather information embedded in "public literature," such as a newspaper article, an advertisement, a comic strip, or a book cover. Then each group presented its work and, in doing so, accomplished the original purpose of reviewing key developments and concepts in the chapter under study.

Students appreciated such efforts and agreed that they had a greater likelihood of learning the material and the teacher was more likely to engage those without much interest in school. First, an activity such as Margaret's study guide design helped students remember better, according to one of the students we interviewed. She described the activity as "giving us a little freedom to use our imaginations."

We asked if she thought that was a good way to handle an assignment such as this.

"It is," she said, "if you have fun, you are more likely to remember the material."

Another echoed those thoughts: "I get things more when the activity is hands-on. I am, whatchamacallit? I have an IEP [individualized educational plan]. I'm having trouble reading, so I get things more if, like, we have hands-on in groups, like in English where we were doing those posters."

We began an interview with another of Margaret's students by asking about classmates who spent more effort disturbing things than learning.

"They just don't have the knowledge to do what the teacher wants," she explained. "They are smart enough, they could do it if they tried. It's just they are smarting off rather than caring about the work."

"Why is that?" we asked.

"It's boring to them." And then she paused and agreed, "School is boring."

"Then why don't you act up as well if it's boring to you?"

"Oh, I'll just sit there; eventually it'll get interesting to me. Like Ms. Waters, that is the most interesting class we have. I do the work quick in there 'cause I don't sit around. She don't have the whole class just sitting there writing or just watching movies. We get irritated at that."

The truth be told, the student was not particularly enamored of Margaret's study guide activity, primarily because she preferred to work by herself.

"I get irritated when someone tells me I'm wrong. I like for other people to be around me when I work, but I want to do it by myself."

But the student was adamant in identifying Ms. Waters as exemplary of a good teacher.

"A good teacher is someone who don't just drag on. She gives us interesting things to do and challenge our brain. She don't just get us out the way."

"So, does Ms. Waters challenge you?"

"Oh, yeah. Here the work we have—I don't think I can do it. But she just keep at you. Other teachers try to be strict and then give us easy assignments, like word searches. We shouldn't be doing that still in tenth grade."

Despite the emphasis on variety in her instruction, Margaret did not believe in using multiple definitions of success with her students. Her ire in working with students who had not traditionally succeeded in school was reserved not for the youth but for the adults who worked with them, adults who substituted a student's making an effort to work for a student's doing the work well. Margaret stressed:

> We must raise standards and stop worrying about how this looks on paper. We're afraid of looking bad on paper if we raise standards. I'm really appalled by the level of standards of teachers. Teachers use kids as an excuse instead of the need to work harder. I'm really annoyed by the level of standards of teachers.

Such tenacity on the part of a teacher was not common in the high school, according to the above student at least. After all, the students were almost old enough to be on their own. It was time for them to take responsibility for themselves. If they were not willing to make the effort to succeed, then a teacher with well over a 100 other students certainly did not have the time to hold their hands. Margaret did not disagree with this conclusion:

> I see it as my job, but I'm in the middle; they've ultimately got to do it.

She simply disagreed with the timing of when it was appropriate to relinquish responsibility. She did not necessarily expect high school students to bring that trait with them to class along with their pencils and notebooks. One of her students—who self-described himself as "when I was young [the previous year], I didn't take school seriously"—was grateful:

> The teacher should say, "I will help you bring that grade up; I will help you and then you have to help your own self." My friend who dropped out got behind and said, "Like I can't make the work up!" Now, like in English class, the teacher is like what I want to have in all my classes. We've had things in there I'm not used to doing. But when I started doing it, she started talking

to me and I started taking it seriously. She say to me, "You too intelligent to stop doing what you working on; you are a good person; you have the knowledge to do the work." She is just a good teacher. I come into her class mad sometimes still and say, "Aw, come on, I don't want to," but I know I will have to do it. If I don't understand it, she will sit down and explain it to me. She will do a problem to show me. That shows me she is really trying to teach me so I can get it on my own. Some teachers give me a big long sheet to do by such and such a day, but interrupt us! I say, "Man, I'm trying to get this done." But Ms. Waters, she different. If she want you to get work done, she won't interrupt us. But if we not getting it done, she keeps coming by, letting us know she wants us to work. If something is really hard, she will stay after school to help. Some teachers will just write notes home, write notes, saying I'm not getting it like I'm supposed to get it. I like to see the teacher will pay attention to what I'm doing. I like that.

If anything, this student was potentially the perfect example of a student who could have succeeded by simply putting forth the effort that most students ordinarily gave. That is, in comparison to his prior behavior in classes, actually finishing assignments was a step that could have resulted in higher grades than the quality of the work might have deserved. However, the student bought Ms. Waters's standards argument:

> When I came to school, I didn't give the effort. I made sure I had a passing grade [a D], but now I'm like, "I need that A, I need that B." I don't want to bring home no more Ds to my mom. I want to be able to read things intelligently. When I have a kid, when my kid ask me a question, and I have to say "I don't even know it," that would be embarrassing. I want to be like "you have to know how to do that."

Referring to this student in particular, Margaret said that was the approach that she took with most low-performing students, the "borderline" ones in her terms:

> He started out playing with me. He would ask to go to the health center, and I realized he wasn't really going there. So I called him on it. I called his uncle. He was shocked that I took the time to do that. Now he knows I care enough about him to stay on

him. But then he started complaining: "The work was too hard." I've found, though, if you set your standards high, students will come up to them. He's not an overly bright student, but not totally incapable. He just takes a longer time to do the work. If I encourage him, he will do it. He needs constant reassurance. My role with him is to reassure him, so that eventually he won't need that so much, so he will gain confidence.

One of the females we talked to earlier noted that not all teachers were willing to devote this much attention to struggling students. She claimed:

> Sometimes teachers treat students differently. They will treat the D people different from the A people. It's like they are helping the A people more 'cause they know they will get farther with them. So they will help them. The D people, they let them go.

Margaret recognized that some students would achieve differently from others. She was "realistic" about this. "Being realistic" was an ubiquitous adjective we heard in interviews that often yielded excuses as to why a student was not doing well and was immune to the interventions of a teacher. In Margaret's case, however, being "realistic" meant that progress toward her standards had to be defined situationally, even though her ultimate standards for success remained constant. On the way to that goal, the benchmark sometimes simply had to be increased attendance:

> The kids who are not doing well in my class don't come to school. Like [one male toward whose empty desk she pointed], I've been on the phone with his grandmother about this. He just acts like he doesn't care about anything. Who knows what the cause is? He is smart enough, but he does the bare minimum. Some days he will work, and some days he will try to sleep. But he knows I won't let him do that. I look at it as at least he has enough drive to get here even though I know I am not going to get his attention. That is the frustrating part of teaching.

A slight woman, Margaret did not wear a red cape. She recognized limits to her influence over students and recognized that outside problems and poor attendance could be potent antidotes to high standards, encouragement, and extra help. The tug-of-war between her needing to do so much for some students to get them to succeed and needing to maintain a life outside school herself was taxing, leading to anger that so much was required of teachers to promote success for all and guilt that she was not doing enough.

From the student side, there was no such dilemma. According to one of the females we interviewed, the way to get students to attend to their classroom chores was "to build a relationship with us, try to act like we do sometimes, have fun, make us laugh."

Yet such a dilemma was the plight of teachers working in this "inner city–like" situation, Margaret acknowledged. Still, she railed against such a label and how often her colleagues used it to justify the poor performance of their students:

> I am sick of being singled out as a district. We're an inner-city school. And people use that as an excuse to do poorly. It makes me angry. I say, "No! We don't want excuses!" I really feel that way. The kids do have special needs. Every kid does. But I don't want excuses. I want the standards to come up. They still need to get an education. I don't want to hear an excuse, and I will do all I can to help them get that education!

JIM EVANS: FOURTH-GRADE SELF-CONTAINED

The following account is told exclusively through the words of Jim Evans [a second-year teacher of the only fourth-grade classroom in a small, nearly 100% minority school], five of his students, and our classroom observation records

JIM EVANS ON INSTRUCTING RATHER THAN DISCIPLINING STUDENTS

This is my second year teaching. Last year, if kids acted up, it was "do something for half a second and you're out." They were testing me and I was the new guy. It is more effective, I've found, to keep them in the classroom. If I send them to the office, they have free rein. They talk to people, they're out of class. In my room, I can keep an eye on them. My lessons don't come to a stop this year. To me, I don't stop for behavior. That way I get more instruction done.

The primary assignment was for the students to write Mother's Day poems, four in all, with two that rhymed and two that did not. Since it was the end of the week, the students also were finishing up several leftover English tasks.

The teacher sat at his desk in the middle of the front of the room. The students sat in groups, their desks pushed together in fours and fives, fanned out around the teacher's. Students individually and steadily came up to Jim for their poems to be critiqued.

At their desks, students appeared to be working purposefully. Jim apparently interpreted things differently, as he quietly and firmly would fill the intervals between critiques:

Charley get to work. Charley? What are you working on? Get moving now. Finish it up.

Kevin, what are you working on? I may have a better idea for something you should be doing.

Aisha. What do you need to finish up? What was that? All right, why don't you get started then?

Nate, get to work. You have two rhyming poems done. You have two nonrhyming to do.

Hector, you can get your journal to me and start on that.

Hector looked puzzled about that statement and finally said, "I don't know what to write." Jim responded, "Think of something you like to do." Another student called out an unintelligible response. "Am I talking to you, man?" Jim admonished with a soft laugh.

From an Interview with Hector:

INTERVIEWER: What do you think of your teacher?
HECTOR: He a good teacher.
INTERVIEWER: Why do you say that?
HECTOR: Because he just about the only one that you don't get screamed at. Other teachers are mean.

From an Interview with Thomas:

INTERVIEWER: What do you like best about your class?
THOMAS: That we have a great time together. Mostly we don't get referrals [to go to the office for discipline].

INTERVIEWER: Oh, yeah, why is that?

THOMAS: We be good.

INTERVIEWER: What makes you want to be good?

THOMAS: If we caught up with everything, he let us play quiet ball.

INTERVIEWER: What's "quiet ball"?

THOMAS: It's a game where we try to get people out, but we have to be quiet playing it.

INTERVIEWER: So you're saying people behave in this class?

THOMAS: Yeah.

INTERVIEWER: What does the teacher do to make this happen?

THOMAS: Because they know he won't take up with their behavior. With other teachers, the kids know they won't do nothing. When they with my teacher, everybody be quiet.

INTERVIEWER: Do you prefer this or would you rather get to play around more?

THOMAS: When the kids do most of what the teacher said.

INTERVIEWER: Why?

THOMAS: Because everybody have to learn; I want to learn, too.

From an Interview with David:

INTERVIEWER: Why do you say people behave in here?

DAVID: You're comfortable in here. You have bumped heads with him in the beginning of the year, but now you have been with him a whole year and you are used to what he do.

JIM EVANS ON THE VALUE OF GROUP WORK FOR HIS STUDENTS

I find on their worst day, the kids still work better in groups. Nine times out of ten I will mix the groups myself. I try to put kids I know will work together plus someone who will need to be dragged along.

From an Interview with Keisha:

INTERVIEWER: Do you prefer doing most of your work by yourself or in a group?

KEISHA: With a partner.

INTERVIEWER: Why?

KEISHA: Because some people might have some answers and you don't, and they will help you.

JIM EVANS ON ENABLING STUDENTS TO BECOME RESPONSIBLE

To me, it's a responsibility thing. Unfortunately here at the school we don't have any positions like student government for kids to be responsible. To me, if I can make them more responsible now, it will help them later on. I put them in charge. I give them a lot of opportunities to be responsible.

As the class period wore on, students seemed to begin constantly moving about the room.

A female near me gathered up the poems she had been writing and moved them to one side of her desk. She then, with a few casual comments to others, went to the back of the classroom to some shelves that had several word-processing laptop computers on them—Alpha ProWriters. She picked one up and carried it back to her desk. She then typed for nearly 20 minutes, entering her poems into an electronic file. Several other students subsequently did the same.

Four students collected at what they call "the big" computer, also in the back of the class. They took turns bringing up their work on the monitor and then printing the material.

Jim came over to me and I asked him about the computers. He laughed and said, "The laptops are for the whole school, but no one seemed to know what to do with them. So I volunteered to take care of them, and that way they're here in the room for my kids to use, as long as they show they can take care of them."

Students also periodically left the classroom entirely. It looked as if they were displaying their work on the walls in the hallway, but there was also a water cooler just outside the door. At one point a third of the class was in the hallway, none of whom had looked at the teacher as they exited and none of whom had received more than a casual sidelong glance from Jim.

Later, with all the students back in the classroom, Jim went over to whisper to a male and a female, and they all walked out into the hall. The trio received no notice from the rest of the class, now teacherless with only myself sitting in a corner.

From an Interview with Latonya:

INTERVIEWER: I noticed you got up and got a computer. How did you know it was okay to do that?

LATONYA: We already know we got to get the computers and start typing what we write. We don't got to ask. He will make the corrections through the big computer; and when we finish, he will keep it in his files.

From an Interview with David:

INTERVIEWER: What do you like best about this class?
DAVID: That we can behave more. We are role models for the rest of the school. We can behave more than the fifth- and sixth-graders.
INTERVIEWER: Why do you say that?
DAVID: At the beginning of the year, he said we had to be the best class in the school. We have achieved our goal.
INTERVIEWER: How do you know that?
DAVID: In the way we communicate and cooperate with each other.
INTERVIEWER: How did you do it?
DAVID: We all worked together to achieve our goal. We all believed in it and we still believe in it.

JIM EVANS ON PRODDING STUDENTS TO COMPLETE THEIR WORK

I have a kid who is highly unmotivated. I stay on him. This marking period he is behind in only one assignment. It's staying on him. Part of it is cutting a deal: "You stay as successful as you can and I will help you." Part of it is letting him fail and then going back to him and asking, "What could we have done to prevent this?" I've had kids making up work from 3 months ago. I remind them all the time: "You still have this to do." To me, that is making them be successful. It makes them more confident about themselves.

Jim left his desk to walk over to one male slouched in his chair. "You didn't finish this," he said. The student offered a response that I could not quite hear. His eyes did not rise to meet his teacher's. "So?" was Jim's reply. The student's gloomy, somewhat raised voice: "It don't make no sense to me." Jim's voice grew quiet as he talked for 20 to 30 seconds, concluding with "tell me what it looks like and what it sounds like." Jim paused, raising an eyebrow. The student paused, looked Jim in the face, and nodded. Jim smiled, said "keep going," and walked away. The student began writing and continued to do so for over 5 minutes, at which time Jim asked all the students to pause in their work for a moment.

From an Interview with Keisha:

INTERVIEWER: What's a good teacher?

KEISHA: Being nice, funny, and sometimes be a little hard on us.

INTERVIEWER: What do you mean by "nice"?

KEISHA: Like, um, helping us out with our work.

INTERVIEWER: What do you mean by "funny"?

KEISHA: Telling jokes sometimes.

INTERVIEWER: And what do you mean by "a little hard"?

KEISHA: Like staying on who have to finish their work.

From an Interview with Hector:

INTERVIEWER: Do you have a lot of assignments in this class?

HECTOR: Yeah, and you gotta, you gotta finish all of them.

INTERVIEWER: What does the teacher do if you don't?

HECTOR: He got a book and he look in it and if you ain't finished. . . . We have something called Success Connection where you stay until 4:00 and finish it all.

INTERVIEWER: Is it a good or bad idea to make you finish everything?

HECTOR: It's a good idea.

INTERVIEWER: Why is that?

HECTOR: Because, um, if you ain't finished at the end of the year, your grades will drop to zero.

INTERVIEWER: What does it take to be successful in his class then?

HECTOR: Get all your work done and stay out of fights.

INTERVIEWER: How does he determine what grade you get?

HECTOR: Uh, you got your attendance and have to have all the work turned in and stay out of fights.

From an Interview with Latonya:

INTERVIEWER: What does it take to be a successful student in this class?

LATONYA: Respecting others, following directions, having fun, participating 100% in every activity.

INTERVIEWER: What do you mean by 100%?

LATONYA: That means if we want to play a game, like quiet ball, we will do every assignment.

INTERVIEWER: Do you have a lot of assignments?

LATONYA: Yeah, but a lot of people don't like to work that

much, but people love to play games. We know we will do fun stuff only if we do all of our work.

From an Interview with David:

INTERVIEWER: What happens if you don't do an assignment?
DAVID: He will make us, if we didn't. We will finish our lessons and we'll have free time if we do it. If you don't, you can do it at Success Connections.
INTERVIEWER: Do you like that he does that?
DAVID: I am glad for the way he teaches. He makes you get it done. If he doesn't want all the students to get done, he might as well not be a teacher.
INTERVIEWER: So what makes a teacher a good one?
DAVID: Well, a teacher who doing they job, which is to teach. He can let kids have fun, but the teacher is not here to make you laugh. The teacher is here to teach you. If you do good, then you can have free time.

On the side wall of the classroom near where I was sitting, there was a cardboard cutout of a fishing net. The net was about 4 feet square and gathered at the top by trawler lines. Above the net appeared the words, "Are you caught up?" Inside the net were different-colored cards, each corresponding to a subject.

JIM EVANS ON PRODDING STUDENTS TO COMPLETE THEIR WORK WELL

I have learned that not all of them are A and B students. But the trick is to give them success when I know they need it. Now, I don't hand it out freely. I make them earn it. I am very consistent in keeping the goals high. With that, early on, the kids were struggling. But by Thanksgiving, I saw a lot of growth. They figured out, "Wow, he's serious." They realized they would get zeros. My standards weren't going to change. For one kid, who really had trouble with vocabulary, I told him we would cut his list down to 10 words. He argued stringently with me that he wanted the full 15.

It is 9:35 a.m. The entire class of 18 students is either writing or talking to the teacher. A female sitting near me keeps looking my way. "Do you write a lot in this class?" I asked out of the side of my mouth. "Or do you do it only every now and then?" She shook her head slowly and rolled her eyes, as only the pre-adolescent can. "We do a lot of writing . . . every . . . single . . . day."

From an Interview with Latonya:

To do well in here, you have to practice. You gotta like learn and play with other people, and know 'em. You gotta study every night and day.

From an Interview with David:

INTERVIEWER: What do you want to do in the future?
DAVID: Be the first Black president of the United States.
INTERVIEWER: Why do you want to be that?
DAVID: Because if I be the first Black president, I would treat people fairly. We would have a Black history test for every student in American history.
INTERVIEWER: Why would you want to have a test?
DAVID: Because I feel students in college don't do enough work. Students in kindergarten need more work. They are doing too much passing, too much passing when people should be held back. They should be held back so you can show them they are not doing enough work!

JIM EVANS ON HIS STUDENTS' ACHIEVEMENT

In the past we had not had any of the fourth-graders passing the state assessment. This year we had one or two pass it outright, and we have a middle group that is so close. I don't think the gap between them and passing is very big and I can see we are making up some of those gaps. My parents are really involved. I have 100% attendance for conferences. The night before the state assessment, I took the whole class to the local buffet for dinner. We had all but one parent show up for that. I don't have the magic word for this, but I have kept parents informed about what's going on. I have sent tons of stuff home and I am constantly keeping them informed about their kids. I invite all the parents to come in and visit class. I definitely have huge support from them, and the kids have made a ton of progress.

From an Interview with Thomas:

INTERVIEWER: Do you feel like you are learning a lot this year?
THOMAS: Yeah, because last year, I couldn't read. Well, I could

but not that good. Not like now. Seeing everybody else read, I started reading good. I go home now and read sometimes.

JIM EVANS ON THE "ON-THE-JOB" ORIGINS OF HIS PHILOSOPHY

What training did I get that influenced how I do things? Well, to be honest, it wasn't in college so much. Actually, before I got this job, I interned for several months at a nearby junior high— Granite Junior High. Do you know about it?

[Note: As it turned out, we did know about this school and describe it in detail in the next chapter.]

5

Granite Junior High School

Our shoes clacked on the marble floor. The sound bounced crisply off the dark, hardwood walls and cavernous ceiling of the 70-plus-year-old school building. Trying to conduct an interview on the run, we were tagging along with the principal as he circumnavigated the building. Even though it was the middle of a class period and theoretically the halls should have been empty, it was also lunchtime. There would be handfuls of seventh-, eighth-, and ninth-graders moving about the junior high. Some would have passes to legitimize their wandering, some would not, and all would "positively, absolutely" have to get where they were going. Adjudication would be necessary.

This meant that the principal had plenty to do. The principal always had plenty to do. What that "plenty" was simply shifted at different points of the day. Before school there were small meetings—with parents, teachers, staff members, students, and the inevitable visitor. The first few class periods provided time to resolve matters left over from the previous afternoon. Lunchtime was spent trying to keep the lid on the steaming caldron of adolescent energy that spewed forth as predictably as Old Faithful. Afternoons would bring new conflicts: "He said, she said," "My child feels her teacher has it in for her," "I need some ideas about how to handle this student in my morning class." After school came more meetings, in the school and at the district office.

Thus we tried to squeeze in one or two of the questions from our carefully crafted "principals' protocol" between the myriad routine crises of the schoolday. Crossing from the main office toward the gymnasium, the principal explained that he was retiring. He was a fit, vigorous man in his early 50s, just into "educational" retirement age (30 years of service and out) and less a victim of burnout than the possessor of a burning desire to continue to grow personally and professionally.

The decision had been long-planned but only recently shared with the school and the community and done in a typically understated way, so much so that teachers still talked about the coming event as if it were a secret. Some in the school held out hope for a reversal. Thus it was with some hesitation that an approaching student spoke to him:

"I understand that you're leaving us," she said with a somewhat furtive tone.

"Oh, I'm not really leaving you," the principal replied, "I'm still going to be around; I'm just not going to be the principal."

With a little more anxiety, the 13-year-old exclaimed, "But what are *we* going to do?"

"Oh, the new principal will be fine," he assured the student.

"But . . . but . . . but what if he doesn't know the rules?" she cried.

There was much more to the student's question than whether the new principal would know about hall passes, detentions, and when to allow pizza parties. To be sure, Granite Junior High School had rules, but the ones to which the girl referred had more to do with academics than discipline, and they were not necessarily etched in stone. Rather they were more ingrained in the minds of the adults and young people—and deeply so, as evidenced by Jim Evans's (Chapter 4) transporting them from his stay at Granite as an intern to his first permanent position elsewhere in the district. They were habits, customary ways of doing things, a set of beliefs and guiding principles for how students, teachers, and administrators expected each other to act with respect to schoolwork—not a list of behavioral "do's and don'ts."

What those rules were and the effects they had on the residents of Granite make up an important story to tell. Located a dozen or so blocks from downtown in a Midwestern city, the school had a mostly poor, ethnically diverse student population whose members were largely succeeding in school—succeeding in the sense that nearly everyone finished their work assignments to the satisfaction of their teachers and students' academic performance on standardized tests compared favorably to that of wealthier students at schools elsewhere in their district. Such results were not surprising, however, to Granite's administrators and teachers. For them, the surprise would have been if their students were not succeeding.

THE "RULES" AT GRANITE

School was all about classwork—getting it done and getting it done with "quality." We found no misconceptions about this anywhere in the building. Everyone agreed that the driving motto of the school was that every student would complete every assignment at a level sufficient to get a B. Students worked on unfinished and unsatisfactory assignments until they were complete and satisfactory, all the while keeping up with new work. There were no zeros to serve as pardons, no detentions that would substitute time served for tasks undone, only "incompletes" and "not yets." Even the end of the schoolyear offered no relief from the press of responsibility. There was summer school until that I (for "incomplete") became a B.

It sounded so intuitively simple to us to run a school based on the principle of completing work. If a task was worth giving, then it was worth doing; and if it was worth doing, then it was worth doing well. This refrain was not a mere slogan to motivate students to do their best. It was a rule that applied to everyone. There would be no Cs, Ds, or Fs; only As, Bs, and Is. Two teachers explained:

> We work really, really hard to not let kids fall through the cracks. We want success for every student. We say to parents, "We'll guarantee success if you get them here." That is one of the strong things about this school, the fact that everyone works so hard to get the entire student population to be successful. We're on an "A, B, I" system. There is no failure. You have to really make an effort to fail. We tell them, "You will do your work." Sometimes that feels like to us, "Who is really doing the work here?" Us or them? That gets real frustrating, when a kid plain doesn't care. But we do work really, really hard; we pound away on that incomplete list.

> If every assignment is valuable and meets my objective for what I'm teaching, then every assignment is worth doing. To let a child settle for not doing it then is out of the question. If they settle for what might be a D, then what objective isn't being met by letting them do that? If they are not in class, they don't get their work done, and they *know* we're gonna be on them.

To us, it really sounded somewhat like an educator's nightmare. There was no closure to an assignment, no test given only once, no point at which a teacher could just say, "That's it; time's up; whatever you've done is what is graded." Instead, students had to keep at it, at everything, until they reached "quality"—a set of criteria for each assignment or test or project that established what would earn a B.

This notion of quality was important. The teachers were concerned that they would fall into the trap of saying "All children can learn . . . something." This turn of the phrase would allow them to toss a lot of students into the grab bag of successful ones who, in fact, were successful only in an individual growth sense and not in terms of over-all excellence. Most of the faculty were neither willing nor ready to do this. A teacher elaborated the thinking behind this approach:

> So what do you do with students having such different academic backgrounds? We, as educators, are always under the criticism for "dumbing" school down for some. But here we're working under mastery learning. That means every assignment has to be done with quality. Besides what good do we do breaking this kid down by saying you aren't as good? All we do then is force them out of school. We tell them they are incompetent. Where's that get our community? The quality of life of the community is enriched by our educating these kids. I see no advantage in sorting and selecting. People say that is not the real world. Well, this is *not* the real world!

Two other teachers cut more succinctly to the chase:

> The key to [student] success is having all work be done at the best level possible.

> We try not to lower expectations. My job is to show the kids what they need to do to be successful in high school and life.

Students maintained an I until they had completed an assignment or a test on which they had done poorly. A grade of B showed that a student had demonstrated mastery. An A required students to do work beyond quality, such as would normally be associated with extra credit. On the wall of one teacher's classroom, a poster defined the grading scale as followed:

A = Above and beyond
B = The basics—you know your stuff
I = Incomplete—you need more time and support

In practical terms, this meant that students only received an A if they engaged in what would be called in most schools "extra-credit" work. Students identified examples of such assignments as working in the computer lab on a class topic, doing library research, writing an additional book report, trying to solve an extended "story" problem in math, or displaying one's knowledge of a subject more creatively than required (via the arts, for instance). They explained that the work always related to the current class content but that it was "over and above" what they were doing in class.

A B grade was synonymous with achieving "quality" on an assignment. To receive it, a student had to meet the standard his or her teacher established. According to students, the standard varied somewhat from teacher to teacher. With respect to tests, some demanded that "all answers" had to be correct, some required getting "15 of 16" right, and some allowed "two or three" mistakes. For writing assignments, students claimed that they were given clear expectations for what would be acceptable, for example, a certain number of paragraphs, a certain number of sentences per paragraph, and a certain amount of detail. Students indicated there was no vagueness about whether they had achieved "quality":

> If you turn your work in and if it is up to standards, they give you a "quality." If it is not, you get "not yet." You know if it's "quality" or not. It's not the teacher's opinion.

These standards, according to teachers, were entirely within reach of most of the students. "We have found out that students work up to what our expectations are," commented one.

All students had to meet the standard of a B or else they kept at it. As Edna Sanders's students had indicated, this insistence on completing work well was frustrating at times, but ultimately for the best (see Chapter 4):

> I think it's good. At the beginning of the year, I was against it. But I've noticed how it helps me. And your grade average is always higher than it was.

We asked teachers about handling this nearly perpetual and mind-boggling array of varied student progress. They were unanimous in their support of the concept of "ABI" but had misgivings about the length of time students had to make up assignments or to reach "quality":

> We do give them too much time. We don't have a cutoff. I have incompletes from 5 or 6 weeks ago. It is not because they can't, but that some choose not to do the work. There is a point where those who choose not to do it should have to do it.

> I like the "ABI." What I don't like is they have all year. I like where they have to get quality on every assignment rather than

just some point value, but sometimes they wait too long to get there.

There is complete teacher buy-in to "ABI," but with deadlines. It doesn't work when a student can make up the first assignment of the year on the last day of school. Every teacher makes an effort to give ample time to do the work. If a student is working, then a teacher believing in "ABI" would extend the deadline.

During the 3 years that we visited the school, the faculty had settled on a somewhat restless compromise on the actual implementation of the "ABI" ideal. The ninth-grade teachers established the end of each marking period as the deadline for assignments ("to get them ready for what they will face in high school"), while the other two grades continued with the more open-ended approach. Additionally, the ninth grade resorted to using Cs and Ds. They still avoided using F. The impending weight of high school routines and the mismatch between life in high school and school life as he envisioned it made the principal keenly desirous of transitioning Granite to a middle school with a 6–8 arrangement, a move that was likely to occur 2 years hence.

The problem, of course, with expecting Bs of everyone was that there were two types of students who fell behind: those who could do the work but did not, and those who could not yet do the work. The former group needed pushing and constant reminders and was the source of considerable adult irritation. The latter group needed more time and help and was the sole reason for the school's being organized in the way it was. As one teacher summarized, "There is a difference between mastering learning and being late and lazy."

Thus the teachers quoted above, as well as those quoted below, did not want to aid and abet the procrastinators endlessly; however, they eagerly accepted the consequences of acknowledging that students learn at different speeds. Teachers therefore constantly juggled their time and patience:

I always am feeling like I am moving too fast for some and too slow for others. Some you don't have to explain the work to. So we have reteaching time. We all have a small reading class [in which everyone in the building is assigned a small group of students to work with on reading], and an aide will catch up some students in that time. And we all stay after school to get students to make up their work.

Our school philosophy is that all kids can learn given enough time. We just look at it as they have not had enough practice, not that they don't have the skills.

The above comments addressed what teachers did after the fact, after it was apparent that a student had not grasped a concept or skill. Teachers also felt that they had to anticipate how well certain students would initially understand a lesson. Thus they concentrated on how they introduced material:

To reach all of the kids? Sometimes I have to lecture 10 to 15 minutes and then have them answer questions about that. Or we will read together, the whole class. Or I will use cooperative learning, which I have to monitor closely so they get all the information. But to say to them read pages 47–49 and answer the questions? I have so many who can't do that; and if they are reading, they don't know what it means. That is the biggest challenge to me. I find I might need to tell them a story first. I like to try to help them see what they're reading as a story.

Despite the frustration of having students who fell behind, especially students who dallied and whose parents did little to check on their assignments, the teachers in this school rarely shrugged their shoulders with an attitude of "what can you do—it's out of our hands." Instead, they looked inward for solutions to reach the unmotivated:

If we give up on them, then everyone has given up on them. They are still children. A lot of our kids are without strong parenting. So it's our responsibility. Who taught me? My parents. Who is teaching them? We form that connection with the students. When do you say enough is enough? You don't. How can you say that you've done all you can? It's up to you. If they have bad parents, we have to step in or we will be unleashing a really scary future. We can't do that.

Until they are responsible for their own education, we are responsible for them. Letting them cop out? NO! We are the parents here; we have to be responsible! If I make being here worthwhile, they're gonna be here. I don't think it's even the nature of the bird to be fired up about learning. Socializing is natural. If we can pique their interest, they will be. I go back to we're the adults; we know they need to be educated. Throw in some fun and let them trust me. Tell them: "We know how to teach you; the deal is you agree to do what I ask you to do; my deal is to ask you to do those things that will let you learn."

They also had to look at discipline in a slightly different way. A teacher offered some fairly irrefutable logic:

A student can't be sent out into the hall. If they are not in class, they will get behind. If they get behind, they don't complete their work. If they don't complete their work, they will have an incomplete.

So, the teacher continued, teachers could not afford to take student misbehavior "personally" and punish a student without thinking about the consequences of that punishment for completing assignments.

Another way of saying that some students were behind was to say that some students were ahead:

Teaching would be so much easier if students were grouped by ability for instruction.

But students were not, so teaching was not. Other provisions had to be made to avoid "downtime" for the faster students. One way was to offer "sponge" activities that could "soak up" the time of students who had finished an assignment. The art was to create activities that extended the students' learning without appearing to be busywork. To lend substance to these extensions, teachers used these as the means by which students could transform their Bs into As.

A similar strategy of providing simultaneous opportunities to catch up and move ahead was in place schoolwide. The last 30 minutes of the schoolday was called R&E, for "reteaching and enrichment." During this time, students who required additional help or time to complete a task went back to their teachers' classrooms; students who were "caught up"—that is, they had completed all of their assignments at the "B" level—could work on extensions, most often in the computer lab or library, to move up to the "A" level. In addition, students interested in music had their orchestra and band classes during R&E. This arrangement found classroom teachers in their respective rooms, having to work with only those students in need of additional time or help.

Teachers and students alike thought it was perfectly normal that some students might require reteaching while others explored the enrichment options. It was a tangible acknowledgment of the truism that people learned at different speeds.

Classrooms were businesslike, to say the least. There was always a task to be done—either a current one, a past one, or an extension. A teacher depicted the tone this way:

> I have a lot of kids who like my subject this year. It isn't because they're getting to play tiddlywinks. I'm nice to them out of class, but in class, it's all business.

If students lost track of where they were, every classroom had a version of an "Are you caught up?" chart on the wall. These varied from the pedestrian—crosshatched tables of names, assignments, and checks—to the artistic—for example, fishing nets with the names of those on top of their work inside the net and those needing to catch up floating around elsewhere on the display.

Enacting these "rules" was a tough job for teachers. It siphoned time and energy from a job where time and energy were already at a premium. A teacher would spend 50 to 80 minutes working with youngsters. Then, during the brief class changeovers, in lieu of taking a breath, the teacher would stand out in the hall reminding those with assignments still outstanding to get them done and recruiting those needing extra help for an after-school session. As for that, teachers would teach all day and then reward themselves by staying past the bell to teach some more.

The teachers used a few "tricks of the trade" to ease some of the burden. For one, most of them used group work in the classroom. Some were quick to point out a distinction between having the students work in groups and doing cooperative learning. With respect to the latter, the school had invested heavily in having the teachers undergo formal training in cooperative learning. Indeed, a certified trainer was a member of the faculty. Cooperative learning followed a rather strict and consistent set of guidelines; for example, assigned student roles within the group, constructive contributions from all group members, and individual accountability:

> In a group of four, I make sure one is a reader so that person can read material for the group. I make sure at least one can be a helper on something. Now, you never group assess. That is always individual.

The difference in group work and cooperative learning? You need tight control, a structured time frame, more supervision, set ways to be accountable, do not let kids hitchhike, and you have time-lines to meet the rubric.

Not all the teachers went this far with groups. In our observations, it was more typical for the teachers to give an assignment, have the students work on it individually in the group, and encourage them to turn to one another for needed assistance prior to asking for the teacher's help:

I do a lot of cooperative work. I try to get them to sit beside someone with a different background from them. And I don't like to put low-achievers by each other. Still, in the small group, the low-achievers get a chance to talk. I do direct instruction for 15 minutes, and then do the cooperative groups. If they don't understand what they're doing, they have help there.

Thus groups increased the amount of help, and encouragement, available:

You can't fail if you show up because the group will make sure you do the work. They force participation by everyone. They hold each other accountable for the work.

The best days I have are when it's loud and they're moving around. I know it's an effective way to teach and learn.

They also structured the schoolday to increase the amount of time available to help students. For several years, this "structuring" essentially was staying after school for an hour or more, well beyond what was called for in the teachers' contract. Burnout was on the horizon. The teachers and the principal therefore had recently instituted the "reteaching and enrichment" period—the 30 minutes at the end of the day referred to earlier. Thus reteaching was formally acknowledged as inevitable and natural, and—more importantly—the responsibility of the school rather than the child and/or parents at home.

Finally, the teachers worked in teams. Four or more of them had the same group of students for all their major subjects. The "or more" referred to special education teachers who joined the teachers in class as part of an inclusion effort in the school. This close collegial arrangement enabled them to devise and apply a consistent set of expectations, to support one another's efforts, and to share ideas about working with students, particularly those who seemed to be having difficulty. The teachers rarely acted on a student problem or considered a redirection in their lessons without consulting teammates. In fact, before we could begin an interview with one teacher, she let us know in no uncertain terms that everything was done from a team approach and that it made no sense to interview her without including the others, especially the special education teacher with whom she team-taught the class.

More significantly, special education teachers became additional resources to improve students' chances of receiving extra needed help. For example, in one eighth-grade classroom we visited, we had a brief glimpse of how two adults could ensure that all students were following along with a lesson. The class in question had been reading a passage from a social studies book. One of the teachers directed the lesson while the other floated around the room to answer questions, offering gentle but insistent reminders to students about the importance of staying on top of their work:

> If you are not with us, you won't be on the bus. Let's all get on board.

> The bus is being loaded. We're taking tickets. Everyone get on board.

Every few minutes the two would briefly confer privately about whether students understood both the instructions for the tasks and the content. They referred to this as a "tag-team effort." During the lesson, *every* child had multiple opportunities to indicate his or her understanding in the presence of one or both of the teachers, and each teacher came through the exercise a little less exhausted:

> Teaming really helps us here. If something is not working for a student, we bring the student in [before the whole team] with their parent and create a program to get the work done.

A teacher new to the school and the challenges of an urban environment, but not to education, was straightforward about where she would be without the help of her peers:

> Teaming makes this school so successful. I would be in the dark without it.

Teachers readily acknowledged the influence of their team members and the value of seeking advice rather than working in isolation. Referring to a colleague who had passed away the previous year, a teacher commented:

> He really understood that kids learn at different rates and paces. When we were overwhelmed, we would always turn to him to see what he would say. He was fond of saying, "When something isn't going right, no one died; let's find out what went wrong and fix it."

Not every teacher in the building could or wanted to "follow the rules." As one teacher explained succinctly, "The bottom line is: This is a lot of work." Estimates varied among those we talked to, but people seemed to believe that most of their colleagues really were committed to what they were doing. They also said that the other ones did not stay around long:

> I would say 80% have bought into the program. There are other people like us in other buildings in the district, but they are in the minority. Here, we're a majority. If you don't get on board, you don't stay.

> We do have some new teachers. We say to them there is no question. This is how we do it here.

But, we wondered, what about a subject such as math? It would certainly be unfair to cast the mathematics teachers as recalcitrant, or as violating "how we do it here," just because their subject matter was sequential and therefore not as amenable to the "ABI" system. It would be equally unfair to force them to adhere to a system that was patently incompatible with a subject based on learning prerequisite skills. Wouldn't it? At least that was the reasoning we used in questioning math teachers about "ABI." Setting us straight, they disagreed:

> I'm fortunate. Our curriculum does have building blocks, but students don't have to master one before the other necessarily. Instead, we do investigations. All of the students can contribute to these real world–type investigations. So, we can move along. It becomes obvious during these when students haven't mastered previous information. That's where extra work comes in so the

kids don't get left behind. I'm not sure how I would handle things if we had a traditional math program.

The "rules," then, applied to all in the school, regardless of age or expertise. It would be misleading to suggest, however, that "how we do it here" was applied rigidly or blindly. Clearly, teachers frequently pointed to troublesome aspects, and compromises such as the one with the ninth grade emerged as a result. However, the core tenet that all assignments worth giving were worth doing and would be done did not find itself discarded with the dirty bath water of the difficulties created by living up to that belief.

THE ORIGIN OF THE RULES

The above portrayal of the school is obviously a snapshot, a snapshot of a school committed to a common goal and to hard work to achieve that goal. But why did a picture of the school happen to look that way and not another? What brought that group of people together in that way at that moment? Such paths are often not easily traced. In the case of Granite, however, three clear landmarks delineated the way—the principal, staff development, and time.

The Principal

Teachers attributed the initial "rules" on which the school was based to the principal. They represented his notions about effective schooling:

> He brought a vision with him that kids are first. He instills that in others. He doesn't fall back on the excuse that they have bad family situations. He truly believes that all of them have the capacity, and we should be always searching for the right kid-based programs.

The principal initiated this search by having the faculty talk about which students were not performing well in school and why this was the case. The focus in these discussions always returned to what the school *could* do to better serve those who had traditionally not done well rather than what could not be done for them.

The principal also stacked the deck, so to speak. In addition to convincing teachers that the evolving ideas about enabling all students to become successful were good ones, he strategically assembled a faculty that was already predisposed to them. This engendered a sense among the faculty that they were special. Indeed, they saw themselves as "handpicked," "strong," and "innovative":

> He has handpicked us as well. My team has been together now for 4 years.

> He just started with a real strong vision and picked a real strong staff. And the new staff members come into teams with things already in place. It's so smooth.

> I came here because of him. I have always liked an innovative principal.

And then, according to teachers, the principal made sure that everyone knew that everyone was expected to support and reinforce the vision. For example:

> Administrative support is so important here. When you have students missing assignments, the administrators don't tell the teachers "It's your problem." They get involved in helping. For a while, it seemed so strange for administrators to be involved in that way.

Staff Development

Educational research does not always enjoy a favored status in the minds of educators. "It's fine in theory but not in practice" is an enduring rebuke of the ability of research recommendations to translate well into effective actions. Others come to mind: "Educational researchers are people who ask to borrow your watch so that they can tell you what time it is" and "If you laid all the educational researchers in this country end to end, they would not reach a conclusion." Such misapprehensions were not present at Granite. The teachers latched onto research and tenaciously incorporated it into their classes, as evidenced in the following teacher's litany of research-based ideas that had been infused into the classroom:

> A lot of things we do make a difference with our kids. Cooperative learning for one. Everyone is accountable for their part in a team. Students can butt heads with the teacher, but when you are with your peers and you have to contribute, that's a lot harder for a kid to refuse. Also with our discipline policy, the

way we treat kids. We have all gone through "reality control theory." That is where you talk to kids; you don't just do things to
them. We ask them, "What are you doing?" "Why did this happen?" "What can we do to make it right?" This is something for
every adult in the building to do.

And rather than regarding these ideas dubiously, teachers felt that the
research legitimated their actions:

Research shows that what we're doing is the right thing for these
kids.

Why teachers at Granite embraced, rather than ridiculed, research
was not too difficult to pin down. Research provided ways to carry
out the vision that the principal and his mostly handpicked staff had
determined to enact. Research, therefore, was a tool to accomplish a
very specific purpose: to ensure that all students completed all assignments with quality. Unlike the child's hammer that turns the whole
world into a nail, ideas such as cooperative learning, quality work,
and reality control theory had a limited but invaluable benefit. They
created conditions under which it was more likely that more students
would complete their assignments. Thus the faculty had a prior reason
to learn about and use research instead of having research thrust upon
them with no more apparent reason than general improvement.

The principal framed the role of research this way: I forced them
to say, "If I believe this, then how can I align my practices with what
I believe?" Research provided the clues about how to accomplish that
alignment. The starting point, however, was not research about best
practice but an examination of what the faculty believed good middle
school education should be.

Thus staff development in the school continually bounced between exploring beliefs and learning how to best enact them. As mentioned, cooperative learning looked like a strategy that fit well with a
number of the "rules" in the school. Thus, over time, everyone had the
opportunity to investigate this. Likewise, the idea of "quality work"
and its value as a target for all children meant that the entire faculty
had to become well acquainted with the theories of William Glasser
and the quality school movement.

Time

Needless to say, reaching the point where a teacher could refer to "how
we do it here" was not an overnight phenomenon. Understandings

about the meaning of the rules were still evolving during our visit. Over time, during team meetings, in the halls, and after school, the faculty developed, tested, and refined their interpretations of the rules. They brought shared and specific meaning to labels that sounded like so much educational jargon: "quality schools," "mastery learning," "cooperative learning," "control theory," "middle school philosophy," and so forth. In the context of the school's daily activity, these ideas came to life and were shared by all.

The centerpiece of the school's staff development was a 3-hour block of time on every other Wednesday morning. The staff had convinced parents to go along with adding time for students on other days to allow the faculty this time when no students were in the building. For 2 years the staff used Wednesday mornings to discuss students, identify student and staff needs, devise plans for meeting those needs, and carry out the plans.

It was inevitable that this development would become a major topic around the district. Other schools wondered why they did not have such an opportunity. So the district instituted the idea for all schools and shifted the block to Monday mornings to better accommodate busing schedules.

It was also inevitable that problems would arise within the district, primarily the whispered complaint that not all of the schools were using the time for whole-school staff development. The central administration's concern about misuse overwhelmed the argument for "good use," and the practice ended for all schools. The principal regarded this as a major, and eventually insurmountable, obstacle to Granite's continued growth:

> They cut it out for everyone. That's a major reason I retired. I couldn't see how we could continue without that released time every other Wednesday. Everybody in the school got it at the same time, and everybody was fresh. That time was a building block for what we did. So many ideas came out of that: the "time-out" room [where misbehaving students went to complete work their classroom behavior was disrupting], approaches we needed to implement our philosophy, the common grading system.

The principal's departure, unfortunately, set in motion a chain of events that resulted in the departure of 75% of the school's regular teachers—a case study in itself, which played out during the last months of our study. Suffice to say that the student mentioned at the beginning of this chapter proved prophetic, and the ensuing clashes between the new principal and the faculty created intolerable circumstances for all. However, the point of this chapter is to describe what a schoolwide "It's my job" approach looked like, how it developed, and what it meant for teachers and students. It is the last of those three purposes that the next section addresses.

GRANITE'S IMPACT ON STUDENTS

If one listened closely to the faculty about students' learning at different speeds and rates, one would conclude that using standardized test scores to assess the progress of such a decidedly nonstandardized population would have been folly. Perhaps it was. Nevertheless, test scores remained the main course at any debate about educational effectiveness in the district.

Interestingly, the state's assessment program lent credence to Granite's efforts. Despite being the poorest of the five junior highs in the district, Granite was second in the number of students reaching a proficient level on the eighth-grade writing assessment. This number was 7% above the district average and 2 percentage points below the state average. Moreover, there was no difference in the performance of its African American and Caucasian students. Such was not the case at the junior high in the district that most resembled Granite in diversity. There, the African American students performed more than 18% worse than the Caucasian ones. The achievement gap between ethnic groups was wider at Granite on the science assessment (about a 15% difference in the number of students achieving proficient status) than it was for writing, but this gap was nearly 95% at the other comparable junior high school. While of concern to Granite's faculty, this gap had narrowed from 30% the previous year.

Given the usual caveats about making numbers say anything one wants them to and needing to add a considerable dash of salt to the results, the school rightly placed modest importance on these numbers, as we do here with our conscious brevity on test score comparisons with what one might call a "control-group" school. However, Granite's educators did acknowledge the results as an indication that they were "on the right track," especially when the differences they saw between themselves and the other junior high were programmatic (e.g., school-based staff development, diligent use of planning time, the "ABI" system, etc.) rather than demographic. Thus the faculty used the test scores as one indicator among many (with the many being derived from their own observations of student behavior and performance) that the school gave all its students an opportunity to succeed at schoolwork regardless of race and that students were making progress toward meeting a reasonable standard of performance regardless of their economic situations.

The teachers and the administrators at Granite believed that they were doing an effective job. They pointed to the test scores as partial evidence but seemed to take greater pride in figures closer to home. Although it was unclear who had compiled the data, the teachers claimed that a disproportionate number of Granite students both made the honor roll once they were at the high school and eventually graduated when compared to the students from the other junior highs in the district.

We do not want to overstate the success of the school. Granite served an economically poor neighborhood, the poorest of all the junior highs, and therefore had its share of troubled students who took out their frustrations in school. As one teacher described:

> Ten to 15% of them are really hard to reach, for whatever reason. Some have a supportive family life, but there are two to three kids out of every classroom. They make the job harder than it needs to be. They take the fun out of it. They are more defiant. Every time you stop, you do lose class time. But that's how they deal with things. It is a learned behavior. It is wanting that attention. A lot of those kids lack in school, and they don't want to be embarrassed. So they do the opposite. They take control.

The principal and teachers had agreed on a common approach to use with such students:

> Here we have a kind of a process. For two to three times in class, I'll ask the student to stop, to not do that. Then I'll ask the student to step into the hall, and then I'll go out and deal with it. After that, we go to the Student Planning Center [SPC—the "time-out" room]. We—the student, me, and the SPC teacher— will write out a behavior plan for the student to follow before coming back to class.

Not surprisingly, the behavior plan focused on completing the work assigned in class. However, the teacher expressed frustration that the process showed only temporary benefits in some of the cases:

Those kids, it's the same ones. It gives me some relief; they're gone that day. I've been here 5 years and never had a kid removed permanently from my class, but there is no place for these kids. There is no alternative except they come back and it starts all over again. They are not fitting into this program. But then I think, if they don't fit in here, I don't think they will fit in anywhere. Broke kids need more help.

So we would be remiss to portray Granite as having all the answers. However, it did seem to have a good number of them. We return to the students we talked to in this last section to testify to this fact.

STUDENTS AND THE "RULES"

We had found that interviews with students worked better if we had also been in a class with them. This brief common experience enabled us to ground our questions with references to the class. For example, we could ask the following:

> I noticed that the teacher would occasionally call students over to his desk and point to a chart, what was going on there?

> In the small group you were in, what did you guys talk about?

> I heard the teacher tell you to see her at R&E and was wondering what that meant?

In this way we could springboard from a specific event to a more general issue with a little more confidence that the student and we were on the same wavelength. We could not tell whether this strategy also made the students feel more at ease with talking to a stranger. Few students showed any reluctance at all.

Below we draw on these comments to let the students share their perspectives on several aspects of schooling at Granite. In turn, they address work completion and the "ABI" grading system. We conclude this section by providing some indications of how representative the students we talked to were of the overall student population.

Students' Reactions to Having to Complete Their Assignments

Four students were decidedly unequivocal in discussing the school's orientation to getting work done:

> If you don't get it done, you can do it later in class, you can do it during R&E, you can do it for homework, or you can come in after school.

> My teacher is extremely crazy. You never know how she is going to act. You just know she won't let you say, "I can't do it."

> In this class, you have to make up all your work. The teacher is always telling us what is missing and when we have to have it in by.

> Some people let their work slide, about 25%; but they do it eventually or they have to come to summer school to do it.

Their comments were reminiscent of the old oil-filter commercial in which a somewhat ominous-looking mechanic assured viewers that they could pay him now for an oil filter or pay him later for much more expensive repair work, but regardless they would have to pay him. Similarly, students would get their work done "now" or "later"— but not "never."

Staying on students constantly did not seem far removed from old-fashioned nagging, an action that our own adolescents rarely greet with favor at home. We were extremely curious, then, about students' reactions to this "rule."

Some felt that without the teacher, they would lag behind in getting their work done:

> I like teachers who keep after me, so I won't be behind. They want you to succeed.

> What I like best is when we get lots of help, help on our work so we can get caught up. A good teacher keep on sticking with you so you can get caught up.

Others saw the prodding as making the difference between passing and failing:

> If they didn't keep on top of me, I wouldn't be passing. I just wouldn't know the things I know.

Still others felt that the teachers' actions helped compensate for students' poor work habits:

> I prefer a teacher who keeps after me to do my work. I misplace
> stuff. It is easier to pace yourself when a teacher is telling you
> what you need to do.

> I tend to slip off and get off the edge. But the teachers here keep
> hounding us so that we can go to high school and college.

Ultimately, students argued, even though the teachers might have gotten on their nerves a bit, the expectations for students were quite clear:

> Some of the teachers do push you a little bit too much, but it is
> good 'cause you can't quit. You got an assignment to do, you
> gotta do it.

Perhaps in the best position to appreciate the benefits of teachers'
refusal to allow students to choose to not complete their work was a
student who had transferred in from the other junior high in the district that was demographically comparable to Granite.

> In the long term, this school is better. It be better. It'll pay off
> 'cause you always did your best. If you miss a question at the
> other school, they let it go. If you went to this school, you would
> have got it right.

Students' Reactions to "ABI"

Students appeared equally as positive about the grading system. Indeed, the manner in which they talked about As, Bs, and Is suggested
that backing up the teachers' constant reminders with the opportunity
to get a B or A was a particularly powerful punch:

> This time I am getting all Bs. I used to get bad grades. With this
> grading system, they made me get all caught up.

Students continually referred to getting their work done "right," a
phrase that, to us, reiterated the school's definition of success as requiring both effort and excellence. Students did not expect to get a
good grade for trying. Instead, they kept trying in order to get a good
grade, as the following three students claimed:

> If you get your work done to quality, you get a B. If it is not qual-
> ity, you get to redo it. I like this system better because if you

don't get it right you get it back. Not in [another school the student had attended]; there you just get a grade.

I don't want to get an F, and with this system you keep doing it until it is right.

It makes me get most of my work done. In geography I had a real hard time with a map of South Asia. He had me redo it two times until I got it right, and then he gave me a B.

Again, it sometimes took a student who had also attended another junior high in the system to appreciate how different Granite was. The following student not only valued the "rules" but also interpreted enforcement of the rules as a sign of the teachers' interest in the students' welfare:

If a teacher let a person get away with a D or E, they shouldn't be teaching. This school is not like that. When I first came here, I didn't understand that. It takes some getting used to. I was like "oh man, I got to go." But my teacher was, like, "No, stay; you can do it." Now I stay caught up; I'm concerned about being caught up. I don't want my name not called when she say, "Who caught up?" That embarrass me, dude.

Several of them, however, were disgruntled about having to do extra work to get an A. These students felt that getting all the answers correct on a paper, for example, should warrant an A rather than a B. But in most of their classes, the only avenue to an A was to work on the extensions referred to earlier:

I like the fact that to get an A level, they make you do extra work and that makes you more ready for college. But I don't like the fact that even if you get all the answers right, you only get a B unless you do the extra work.

While the above student recognized that doing extra work might have some payoff in the future, the following three saw no such redeeming qualities:

I don't like the A-level program. You have to do more work. You can't get an A just by doing well on tests. You need to do extra-credit work.

I don't like the A-level policy. If you do good, you should get an A.

That's what I hate about here. At another school, if I stay caught up, I would get an A. Here, you do extra work to get a A.

A Look at the Student Sample, from Their Own Descriptions of Themselves

As with the teachers, students described many of their classes, particularly the major ones, as being purposeful. Apparently the incessant attention to completing work made it difficult to get by with not doing so. For example, after listing the times when students could make up needed work, the youth whose comment concluded the previous section added, "but we don't have to do that often because the whole class gets their work done early."

"Why is that?" we asked.

"The kids just don't goof around in here."

Eighth grade? The height of hormone-restricted attention to anything not of a social nature? "Why don't they goof around?" we wondered.

"She make it fun. It's how she talks about things and describes things. She is always comparing it to other things. It is like she is making up metaphors."

"How about an example?"

"We were studying a magnet. She compared it to an ice cube where the atoms were scrambled up. The domains got changed."

A little lost by the comparison, we moved back to why the class did not "goof off."

The student continued, "She even bugs you in the hallway. She is always going over your grade, telling you what assignments you are missing. She comes up to you personally to tell you what is missing."

Metaphors? Domains? Perhaps it was wrong to wonder whether we were talking to a typical student just because a young person easily tossed such words into the conversation—correctly. However, such specialized classroom terms rarely found their way into adolescents' casual conversation. In fact, we were easily startled when a student would respond to a "yes/no" question with a polysyllabic word other than "mm-hmm"; "yeah" or "nah" were the predominant favorites.

We wondered, therefore, about the backgrounds of these students. We had asked teachers whose classes we had observed to suggest interview participants who represented the spectrum of performance and behavior in the class; and we had the opportunity to identify likely candidates from our watching the class. But still, one had to question how unbiased our unscientific sample really was.

In the above student quotes, there were a few references to students having previously received bad grades or shown a tendency to slack off in getting their work done. Such references may or may not have actually identified the student as marginal in terms of previous school performance. Others were a little more direct in assuring us that students, irrespective of their previous success in school, were united in their acceptance of "how we do things" at Granite:

"My friends and I hate school."

Okay, we thought. "So how are you doing in school?"

"I used to get Is. We don't really get As here. I'm trying to get up to Bs."

"And what does getting a B mean?"

"It mean you're getting it done good enough to pass it."

"What happens if you don't get it good enough?"

"You do it over until you do."

"How many times do you do it over?

"As many as it takes to pass. I got most of my work made up now [mid-May]. It has to be made up or if it gets to the end of the year, then I have to go to summer school and pay $5 for each day I have to go to make it up."

"Why did you get so many Is earlier in the year?"

"I guess I don't care for work, so I don't do it. I put it off until the end."

The way the student spoke about "doing work" made it seem more like a ritual than a learning experience. That is, we were suspicious that the emphasis on completing work had superseded the ultimate goal of learning. Apparently, our fears were unfounded; combining work completion with quality negated that possibility.

"Are you learning much in your classes even though you don't like school?"

"Yeah."

"Why do you say that?"

"Because even though you don't get it, the teachers help you out to make sure you understand. They work with you and explain it to you."

Another student, the one who earlier claimed to occasionally "slip off and get off the edge," offered a final ringing endorsement:

This school has the best education in the state. They care about us. They make sure we have it down pat. They are willing to work with us one-on-one to get it right. I know I am better prepared for high school because of that.

CODA

We left the school impressed with the fact that the rules people talked about so incessantly were instructionally inspired. Obviously, the staff concerned itself with discipline as well. The creation of the Student Planning Center was testimony to that. But even that behavior-focused element of the school's operation concentrated on keeping those sent there caught up on their work. Several teachers and the principal told us more than once that there were some students who preferred the tightly structured atmosphere of the SPC precisely because it was the one place where they actually finished their work.

Still nagging in the back of our heads, though, was the question: Who was really learning to be responsible here? The students or the teachers? If the teachers continually stayed on the students to do their work, when would students learn to work without that push? We posed this to one of the teachers. We remember the response, properly chastened:

Adults are responsible *until* kids see the value of getting an education. If they don't see the value, they aren't going to take responsibility—neither now nor when they are on their own.

6

Ridgecrest Elementary

We really try hard to help kids slipping through the cracks. My goal is that I want the kids to be on grade level in reading. The majority is at 1.5 right now (in mid-January). My goal is for them to be 2.5 by the end of second grade. I push them really hard. I work them very hard. I don't give them a lot of downtime.

High expectations? This teacher's goal, if realized, would be the envy of most second-grade teachers who work with large numbers of poor children. In fact, a widely accepted assumption of much national education policy is that enabling such children to read at grade level in their early years is the cornerstone of subsequent academic success. Thus the teacher's ambitions mirrored well the aspirations of early-literacy advocates.

What we learned quickly about Ridgecrest, however, was that high expectations were rarely high enough for long; and we feel compelled to point out that the above teacher taught resource room children, not regular education students. She continued:

My goal is to get them *all* out of special education. They may think they can't do it. I won't make them do what they can't do, but I do want to push them, to bring them up higher. It's hard to get out of special education because of the standardized testing. When they do it, they feel really proud.

Her expectations were not unique, the private mission of a maverick special-needs champion. Within this Eastern U.S. urban corridor school of nearly 600 children (divided almost equally between minority and majority students—a quarter of whom received free or reduced-price lunches, almost 20 percent of whom were in nongifted, special education classes, and over 10% of whom lived in non-English-speaking homes), such a goal was spectacularly ordinary in its prevalence. Staff, students, and parents aimed high for each child in their diverse student population. As the principal explained:

I want to give an explicit message. When I walk in, or a visitor walks in, I do not want them to be able to distinguish special ed and regular ed at all in terms of the learning environment. If outsiders can tell the difference, the children will, too.

Symbols of this emphasis on excellence appeared throughout the school. Slogans, banners, certificates, artwork, classwork, and photographs met the eye everywhere, all touting the recent achievements of students, teachers, staff, and parents. The principal made sure that everyone who entered the building encountered the emphasis on excellence immediately, especially in her office. As you sit there as a first-time visitor, you cannot help but notice the computer banner that stated: "The standard is excellence." Also prominently displayed on the wall was a picture of a mountain with three arrows marking different elevations along its slope. When asked about the mountain, the principal launched into a rapid-fire critique of the goal-setting process in education:

Educators are all over the place in trying new things without often assessing where they are in accomplishing them. One of my bugaboos is people changing goals without first really assessing whether they had accomplished their prior ones.

Coming back to the picture of the mountain, she noted that the school goal was the summit of that mountain, which represented "all kids succeeding." The other two arrows, located farther down the mountain, represented intermediate goals. There was a base camp "with all the students getting ready for the climb" and a middle camp "where 80% are succeeding and climbing." She indicated that the school was somewhere around middle camp and that they would continue on the path until they all reached the summit. The principal even used the mountain graphic in her pep talk to the staff in the fall and assured them: "We can make it to the summit; we just need to stay focused."

To say that having high expectations for its students was characteristic of the school would have been an understatement; and after listening to her, her staff, the students, and parents, you had the distinct impression that no one regarded the summit as impossibly idealistic. Our sense was that the majority of the staff routinely expected exceptional performance—from everyone: themselves, the students, and the parents. Indeed, repeatedly in our interviews the word *excellence* emerged as participants' succinct summary of the school's primary focus. As a parent commented: "This school is a community of learners; complacency is not tolerated."

This chapter attempts to communicate what excellence meant to members of that community, how this goal infused the day-to-day activities of the school, what the psychic costs of pursuing excellence were to staff and what some of the in-place supports to counter these were, and how this pursuit affected students' school performance.

IN SEARCH OF EXCELLENCE

We asked a parent to use one word to describe Ridgecrest.

"Excellence," she replied, with no hesitation.

We repeated the question to the next parent on our interview schedule.

"Excellence," she replied, with no hesitation.

A staff member followed the parents into the small cubicle we were using to talk one-on-one with members of Ridgecrest's school community. "Your one-word descriptive summary of the school?" we inquired.

"Excellence," she replied, with no hesitation.

A student offered only a minuscule variation to the growing monotony of this refrain.

"One word you would use to describe your school?"

"Excellent," she replied, with no hesitation.

No one we talked to disputed this depiction, and no one felt excused from the demands. Everyone seemed to understand that their every action should exemplify the best they had to offer in whatever task they were doing. This expectation extended to visitors, whom the principal always invited to lead the school in the Pledge of Allegiance, via the intercom, as a means of alerting the entire school to the outsider's presence in the building and having the students hear multiple models of respectful behavior. Never had we felt more back in school than at that moment, hoping desperately that words and memories would not fail us. We saw and heard—and experienced—no confusion about the expectations for the building's residents.

Expectations for the Staff

Educators and policy makers often toss around a salad bowl full of reform terms: site-based decision making, standards-based curriculum, performance-based assessment, and so forth. From the student point of view, however, so much of education is "luck-based." That is, the quality of their education hinges directly on how lucky they are to be assigned a particular teacher. Ridgecrest's principal saw this condition as "my first major clean-up piece":

> My thing was that I have a responsibility to children to not play roulette. I have to have all my teachers accountable to children. We don't have enough teachers to go around as it is, so we have to upgrade the ones we have.

Upgrading partially meant providing support to staff members to enable them to do their jobs in the best interests of children, much of which is described later in this chapter. It also meant looking for the kind of person that might do best in the school:

> I need people to be here who want to be here. I tell them the truth in screening sessions. I need to find out about the person. It's my belief that I can teach them how to teach; I can't teach someone to be an advocate for children. That's what I'm looking for. Also the work ethic in this building is very important. I've got to know: Are you coachable? If you can't take feedback, you can't work here. You will get data about students all the time. But there is nothing we will ask you to do, that we won't do. That is not in the past tense. If we need to go in the classroom and teach to show them what to do, then we do it.

Knowing about the principal's unflagging penchant for continual improvement, and thus fearful of a polite reprimand, we nevertheless inquired whether the principal's standards for work performance were too high. She responded:

> Are my standards too high? I don't think so. People want to rise to their highest level. It's a matter of giving them the tools to do that. You cause stress if you don't give them little by little how to do that.

Staff—including the teachers, education assistants, and office and maintenance workers—and parents understood well that every ounce of a faculty's energy should be devoted to making sure that every student succeeded. One of the education assistants explained:

> You can't give up on a child. Maybe that is just me being stubborn, but everyone has something to offer. Everyone has a strength and you work with it.

Not only was the staff committed to working diligently with every child; they also argued that there was no point at which they would become smugly satisfied with their students' accomplishments. As one teacher said:

> We set goals for students and once we accomplish them, we set higher goals. That broadens the thinking of teachers. It doesn't come overnight. It does recharge us and keeps us going.

The teachers, as did the ones at Granite, found themselves turning inward to find the avenue to success with each student:

> We approach the difficult kids as not what's wrong with them, but what do we need to do to help them. We treat them like they are our own kids.

Another teacher was more specific about her understanding of what it took to achieve success for each child:

> We have learned how important it is to know your students personally. I once believed people to be born with intelligence and quickness. Now I believe that it is experience, motivation, and expectations. I used to use the word *smart* without really knowing what I meant. Now, there is a lot more "you can do it" talk in my room. If you say they can succeed without doing everything you can, some will fall between the cracks. Children learn more of what they teach to others; students explain differently than I do. If one thing doesn't work, try something else.

A parent underlined the indispensable role that the adults in the classroom played in communicating expectations to students and in enabling students to meet those expectations:

> If the expectation is there, and the effort is put forth in getting that skill taught, they're sponges. They soak it up. If the expectation is not there, kids sense that. Here they definitely have high expectations set. In too many other places, you see kids just throw in the towel.

Expectations for the Students

Ridgecrest prided itself on having high expectations for students. Having high expectations, however, could have had many nuances. For example, Lipman (1998) detailed how a school that emphasized the success of all students actually maintained one set of expectations for low-income and minority students and another for the more well-to-do majority students. School staff there expected the former to do their work energetically and the latter to do their work well. Ridgecrest's staff wrestled continually with how to promote both effort and excellence. One staff member made the following comment:

> Effort is everything. We don't believe that kids are either bright or not bright. Our job is to channel their energy and effort so that all of them can learn.

And the principal had established four types of certificates that she awarded to students for their quarterly performance in the school: "Honors" for students having all As in their subjects and 1s for their effort; "Achievement" for students having all As and Bs and 1s and 2s; "Perseverance and Improvement" for students who improved in three subjects or in social behavior and went down in no more than one subject; and "Excellent Attitude and Respectful" for students who demonstrated excellent social skills. Taken together, the statement and the recognition categories suggested that while the school symbolically sought academic excellence, some students could have become successful solely by being "good citizens," thereby allowing the school to take an unwarranted pride in its accomplishments.

It had to have been tempting in working with a diverse student population to also have diversified what people would celebrate as success, and the different acknowledgments of students' actions made this a possibility at Ridgecrest. However, to settle on this depiction of the school would have contradicted the bits of evidence presented earlier, such as the goals of the special education teacher mentioned at the beginning of this chapter. Moreover, teachers made sure that we understood that solid academic performance was the goal for all students:

> I have high expectations. Even with these kindergarten students, I want all of the kids reading and writing. There is no reason why they shouldn't be. I will not say any one child can't get where another one can. I won't say that.

A parent picked up on the effort and excellence theme and, in doing so, married the importance of students' doing their work, doing it well, and doing it respectfully.

Students know what is expected. Homework is not an option. Students must do their best. They must do over sloppy work. Respect is [also] the rule. It is clear to my son that he needs to respect his teachers and other students.

The adults bombarded students with the message that they all were expected to work at high levels. The message was not lost on the students whom we interviewed. Effort and excellence appeared inseparable, according to a fourth-grade student.

If something is hard, I ask the teacher and keep on trying until I get it right. The teacher wants you to get it done. No homework, no recess. She is very strict about reading. If you don't finish an assignment, she gives it for extra homework. I keep on trying, reading it over to try to get it. Every day classwork and homework are checked. The principal and teachers always tell you: "Read! Read! Read! And do your best in everything." The principal says, "Excellence equals a good student."

Another nuance to having high expectations for students is whether all students are to be held to the same standard of excellence. The above adults seemed adamantly to advocate an absolute standard for student performance. They wanted all their students to reach a certain skill level by the end of a year's sojourn in their classes. It was not surprising, however, that there were a few teachers who took exception to this point of view. They countered that teachers of diverse students had to be "realistic." "Being realistic" meant adopting a relative standard of student progress, one that used a student's own starting point as the basis for determining progress:

I look where everyone is when they come to me and then try to get them as far as I can. It is difficult when you have children who are 2 years behind grade level to get them to grade level. So I look at everyone and try to challenge everyone. I try to find time to give everyone a push, and I push them all. I do have high expectations. I can find something everyone can work harder on. I look at what a student might be able to do. I differentiate between capability and potential. Now, I will pick some areas of the curriculum where I think everyone can do this. I would like them all to get it, but . . . (*shrugs*). I'm big on potential, on tapping potential. I get a sixth sense of where kids can be.

Another teacher echoed this notion of relative rather than absolute excellence:

> My bar is different for each child. But I am always pushing to see what the bar should be for each of them. If their work is not satisfactory, I make them redo it. I also want to find out why [it wasn't], and modify and change the program if it is not working.

Ridgecrest staff clearly strove to combine effort with excellence—and with respect—but they were not so unified on what excellence meant in academic terms. Rather than leave the definition of what high expectations meant to individual teachers to determine, the school had just begun trying to codify standards for each grade. This effort was being piloted in the fifth grade, as one of those teachers explained:

> We have a set of clear standards for the kids [at fifth grade]. They need to know their times tables, know the Preamble to the Constitution, write a five-paragraph essay, know a rationale for doing math problems, be of service to the school and their classmates. We also have a perfect homework list, and last month all the kids met it.

The initiative started at this grade because the students would be moving on to middle school and the teachers wanted them to be academically prepared for this transition. The rest of the school planned to observe the fifth grade's experiences in teaching, learning, and assessing these goals and then follow a similar process themselves.

Expectations for the Parents

The principal expected parents to play a huge role in their children's educational lives—in the building and at home. The principal did not envision this involvement as being limited to holding bake sales and chaperoning field trips:

> It is a dream of mine to make parents part of the curriculum movement. I want to seriously engage parents in planning the curriculum of the school.

The school received a grant from a local corporation to initiate this dream. The grant allowed the school to arrange a meeting between parents and teachers to begin to figure out how to plan school programs cooperatively and constructively.

Apparently the principal was as unrelenting with parents as she was with staff and students. A teacher observed:

> With parents, she'll drive to their home and pick them up. She tells them there is a reason why your kids do what they do, and that's your job to work on. She's out there picking them up.

The assistant principal underlined the school's expectations:

> Parents tend to take more pride at Ridgecrest, but we expect 100% participation. We set that expectation clearly and ask for their help behind the scenes. We have a parent participation tree [apparently names go up whenever someone comes to the school for an event or activity]. Last year we had 99.2% participation. The principal even invited the nonparticipating parents in for a meeting to discuss ways we could get them involved.

Parents, like their children, had gotten the message. As two acknowledged:

> The principal has this motto that there will be 100% participation. That could mean sending in tissues, but this school wants parents to know what's going on with their child's education.

> They involve the parent in homework. We have to sign off on a sheet every night. You get to where you are setting time to do homework. You see if your child is struggling right away. There is everyday involvement.

Interestingly, despite the current emphasis on the benefits of parental involvement in low-income schools, Ridgecrest staff said that parents were crucial to student success, but not necessary. We hesitate to say that was how a good many of the people we talked to felt, but that in essence was what they were saying. Obviously the students would be better off with adults in the home playing an active role in their education. No one denied that. However, neither did anyone say that as educators they could not do their job if the parents were uninvolved. Teachers apparently saw the lack of parental support as an aspect of students' lives for which those at school would have to compensate:

A child needs parent support. If he or she has it, then they can go further. How I feel is this. I love parents to come in, but I have some who are not involved. So I try to do as much as I can to compensate for that.

The family is enriching. You have to go on the expectation that you're not going to get help from them. Poor parents sometimes have to work three jobs. So that's when you get volunteers to come in to help. You need to do something to fill in.

And, as the principal remarked:

In this school, one of my personal benchmarks is I don't want to debate that we shouldn't do this or that because it should be done in the home. If it has to be done for children, we will do it. That's where it boils down. That's conservation of energy. We could spend it on going back and forth on who should do what, or just do it.

A CULTURE OF EXCELLENCE

Culture, defined simply, is "socially shared and transmitted knowledge of what is and what ought to be, symbolized in act and artifact" (Wilson, 1971, p. 90). The above three sections should be convincing about the extent to which members of Ridgecrest's school community individually shared values about educating children and agreed on how a school should operate in support of those values. To say that these shared beliefs actually had coalesced into a distinctive way of doing things (Deal, 1985), however, one would have to see and hear these values come alive. Otherwise, the verbal affirmations would become suspect—more superficial and less substantial. Thus what people in the school did each day had to reflect what they said in the interviews in order for us to be comfortable in asserting that, in fact, Ridgecrest had created a culture of excellence within its walls.

We offer three sets of evidence that the staff and students at Ridgecrest in fact "walked the walk" of excellence and effort. The first is the assistant principal's introductory remarks to a meeting of parents who were considering enrolling their children in the school. The second combines a teacher's definition of what made a lesson successful with a description of how the students in the class demonstrated their success. The third is more ephemeral and highlights the language that staff and parents used to depict the overall atmosphere of the school.

Introductory Remarks at a Prospective Parents' Meeting

We heard the messages about what was important in the school repeated consistently and continually in public forums. The staff thereby
created a form of accountability for themselves by frequently identifying routine practices that others should expect to see in the school.
This phenomenon was exemplified during one of the periodic pro-
spective parents' meetings that this magnet school held, this one conducted by the assistant principal. She began by describing what parents might expect to find in a typical classroom at Ridgecrest:

> Number one, charts are everywhere. These are designed "to help
> make students individual learners" and provide a record of stu-
> dent progress. Number two, there are only tables in the class-
> room, no desks. This is designed to encourage students to work
> in groups. Even teachers don't have desks! This is to communi-
> cate that teachers are part of the learning community. Number
> three, there is a designated meeting area, often carpeted, where
> the class can go to have whole-class discussions. Number four,
> you will see lots of student work displays. This work is original
> design, not color by the numbers kind of thing. We want to en-
> courage individual thinking and creativity. An example of that
> are the students' different views of turkeys that you see around
> the room. [Students had collaboratively designed a turkey poster
> using readily available materials at home. There was a great vari-
> ety of materials on display, from cloth to food (e.g. different pas-
> tas) to water colors.] Number five, there are grade-level themes
> that cut across the curriculum. Number six, we also believe in
> heterogeneous grouping, unlike what you might encounter in
> some of the other elementary schools. This is a central part of
> the Bank Street model. Number seven, we also make use of a
> staff development person who works with the teachers to plan
> their instruction and coordinate work across classrooms. Number
> eight, we make use of lots of learning trips. We see these as inte-
> gral to the learning process, and we go to a great deal of prepara-
> tion in the classroom before a trip to prepare the students.

The question-and-answer period that followed gave the assistant
principal additional opportunities to publicly reiterate aspects of the
school's operation that we had heard about in private, including the
following exchanges:

> PARENT: Do you have a traditional grading system?
> ASSISTANT PRINCIPAL: Yes. We have report cards for grades 1
>   through 5, and we do conferences in kindergarten. Parent

participation in this process is key to us. We work very hard at that. Our goal last year was 100% participation. We achieved 99.2%. We met with some of the less active parents, and our messages were that parents are the first and foremost teachers. Kids really flourish when their parents participate.

PARENT: When do you group students [by ability] for instruction?

ASSISTANT PRINCIPAL: It doesn't happen here between classes [no tracking], but it does within classes. Students are always working in small groups. For example, we do literature circles where students discuss things they have been reading. Sometimes the class will read a common piece, and other times there will be unique assignments.

A Classroom Lesson

Of course, the assistant principal's comments were still words, even if they were offered publicly. It was possible that the school simply was good at public relations and did not really adhere to the ambitious educational agenda the public statements described. The second set of evidence concerning the development of a culture of excellence at Ridgecrest came directly from the classroom. In the section on student expectations above, we indicated that the school actually focused on excellence in both academics and interpersonal relations. The two seemed completely entwined in the mind of a particular third-grade teacher who offered a somewhat flustered reaction to our question about how she determined whether a lesson was successful:

> Oh wow . . . something like about what happened today [in the class we observed]. They had to put together a project culminating in a lot of skill building. Not only being cooperative and helping each other, but also they wrote titles [to books] and had to correctly put the letter they wrote in the correct format, and the way they ask questions that would require thought. If the skills are there, that's success. I was clapping for them because they showed interactional skill-building information.

A brief period during the morning's activities in this third-grade classroom revealed a couple of subtle but distinct ways in which the teacher tried to reinforce and model this combined emphasis on learning and interpersonal skills. The class was transitioning from math to reading—somewhat artificially, according to the teacher—to accommodate our visit to the classroom to see a language arts lesson. The teacher began the switch by saying, "I apologize for stopping your thoughts on math, but it is time to clean up and come to the meeting area."

The meeting area was in front of the chalkboard. It contained a rug and some benches. As the students gathered, there were only whispers among them.

The teacher continued, "I really appreciate the math scholars who completely cleaned up their tables so the literature circles can go there. I know it was hard to stop. You did a wonderful job of sharing in your math groups, and I heard all the claps for each other [given in response to making a substantive contribution in the groups]. I want to congratulate you."

The students then clapped for themselves, proud of their math work and their behavior.

The "Feel" of the School

Finally, there was a mysterious side to Ridgecrest's culture. People said that they could *feel* it. Perhaps this sense was simply the product of the myriad opportunities one had to see and hear the school's values in action. However the effect was created, a clear idea of what the school stood for was embedded deeply. A kindergarten teacher said:

> I have never said to the children "I want you to do this." It is something they sense. If they have worked on something, they know they can do better. Kids know. You just have to get that across.

A fifth-grade teacher explained:

> I'm always looking for more from the kids. The principal has high expectations, and the kids sense these high expectations. Most will rise to them. It's human nature to do that.

A couple of parents added:

> The people here have a real enthusiasm and passion for what they do. My kids feel loved and appreciated here. They know people care.

> The staff and the administration try to include us. It is like a whole family. Everyone has to be embraced. They teach more of

moral behavior. It is about how you would want to be treated. There is a lot of respect, and something seems to happen. A whole class gets affected. They try to nurture the whole class.

An education assistant elaborated on this feeling of family:

We are the Ridgecrest family. We're working together. That makes it a unified atmosphere. When I moved my kids here, it struck me that everyone was happy here.

A fourth-grade teacher continued:

I wanted to come here to work because of the family atmosphere. The parents, students, teachers, and administrators all work together. It is also very child-oriented. It is unique and special. There is enormous support for my work. The administrators came and helped me set up my room [at the beginning of the year]. The reading specialist worked with me on how to use the books. The staff development person meets with us weekly. She just helped us develop a rubric for book reports. She helps with things from teaching to paperwork. The grade-level team meets weekly—we share information, plan trips together, and they are always willing to help. There is always professional development available to help you. For example, I got some help to deal with a visually impaired student in my class. It is a home away from home. We provide love, experiences, and educational opportunities.

The principal wanted people to know that they were in a school that felt very different from others they had experienced:

We get a constant in-and-out of students in our school, although it is mostly in. We are always seeing the contrast of what students are like when they come in from another place. They typically are low in skills, although that is not a problem for us; but they are also low in their attitude or approach to work. I tell them: "We're happy to have you here, but you are in a different place now." [As an example], I said the school is going to be quiet this year. I thought, "How do I present it so it is not suppression?" But I needed a place where people were calm enough to see the beauty of the environment and respectful enough not to disturb others.

THE PRICE OF EXCELLENCE

Our depiction of Ridgecrest might appear to suffer from hyperbole. Indeed, literary convenience often causes researchers to inaccurately attribute characteristic aspirations, attitudes, and actions of individuals to the school as a whole. Statements such as "Ridgecrest stands for . . . ," "Ridgecrest's teachers emphasize . . . ," and "Ridgecrest staff members expect . . . " potentially masked underlying differences.

At Ridgecrest we found no one unfamiliar with the pursuit of excellence and what it meant for the lengths staff were to go in educating children. In this, hyperbole and reality joined hands. However, given the demanding environment of the school, it was perhaps no surprise that there were differences of opinion among the faculty about whether this pursuit was ultimately advisable and sustainable. The constant push for better results, closer connections, and appropriate practice exacted a psychic price on some of the staff.

In this section, we first present how several staff described the costs for them of working in such a school. The next section then portrays the system of supports that other staff said the school had in place that prevented the drive to excel from crashing in on itself.

One of the teachers we talked to claimed:

> Not everyone is rowing in the same direction here. As a whole, we are on target. We all want the same thing. But there are several who have their own agenda.

This was not new information to the principal:

> The staff have said to me that the people who want to be here also want to meet the standards we have set. However, in the 3 years I have been here, I have grappled with something. People have said to me, "You are intimidating." When I heard it first, it was surprising. I have a strong passion. The energy of a passion can be overwhelming. I have tried to get on the other side of that feeling, and I have had people who use that as an excuse for not performing. The paradox is that I am one of the most flexible people. You can do what you want *if* you work your heart out and have standards. My top-performing people enjoy the highest level of freedom. People, I think, really believe I am fair: Everyone gets my feedback. It is not about anything but the work and the children.

But, as at Granite, the work was hard. Some staff grew weary of maintaining the constant push to demand and meet high standards for student performance and, then, raising the bar so that the effort to excel could begin anew. So, having suggested that excellence had become woven into the daily fabric of the school, we must also add that people often noted that demanding excellence was personally demanding. Within this culture of excellence, staff members worried about becoming burned out from the constant press to expect more, teach more, and learn more. One teacher said:

> The principal encourages us to do well, but that puts too much stress on us. The downside of excellence is teacher burnout. I do have another life. You have to have a balance, and so I don't always feel listened to.

Another staff member concurred:

> Teachers have spent a lot of time in staff development meetings relieving themselves from the stress. No teacher has enough planning time, but they are getting the job done. But given the requests for time, you feel like what you do is never enough.

The upshot was that not everyone who taught in the building could maintain the required level of effort:

> We tend to lose staff because the principal is so demanding. Sometimes she is so involved with her ideas that she is not real flexible with people. She thinks she is open and right. She does get on people a bit much. She is so into excellence. She wants dialogue but sometimes is afraid to do it.

IN SUPPORT OF EXCELLENCE

Given this undercurrent of unease about the toll of taking on the responsibility of enabling all children to work hard and well, we looked more closely at how the staff maintained their effort and growth. Most of the staff argued, as did the following teacher, that they were not alone in the pursuit of excellence for all children:

> There is great support in this school. We have a principal, and an assistant principal, and two reading teachers who know every kid in this building. That means there are less children that can fall through the cracks. If anyone asks for help with a child, they try to get it for them.

It was apparent that the principal recognized that being demanding required support—for all members of the school community. There were several important sources of this support within the building: the principal herself, professional development opportunities, the presence of education assistants in each classroom, and establishing performance standards for students at each grade.

The Principal

In response to how the principal set the tone for the school, a kindergarten teacher replied:

> Her expectations. It is something you sense. When you're working all these hours, she's here. You see everyone pushing themselves.

Another teacher claimed, in response to our question about whether most faculty were in agreement with the school's approach:

> Most are. They didn't always feel that way. She pushed too hard at first. We both have this in common. It's like with kids—you need to turn things over to them and back away. We don't have the same feeling now that we had in the beginning. We have gained more respect. My respect for her deepens each year. She is so intelligent and understanding. I'm a maverick, and she is very supportive. Her presence in [one of our] workshops helped reduce resistance of the staff. She communicated to teachers the value she placed on it.

Three of the education assistants were very clear about the primary stimulus for the building's atmosphere—the principal—and characterized her leadership style as a composite of a positive attitude, clear values, consideration, relentlessness, and modeling.

> She is very positive about what she wants. She has very strong values: Every child will succeed; we will encourage a nurturing environment; we will give them positive experiences. We all have the same goals at this school: to make children succeed. We believe that every child can learn. They just need a key to open the door to do it.

Sometimes teachers are overwhelmed. There are lots of different things thrown at us. But she is a great person. She appreciates us. Last month we all memorized a poem [for a special program], and everyone had a part in it. We all got notes of thank you from the principal. She shows she knows we are here. She puts in 110% effort.

We have a loving principal who drives and pushes to make sure these kids have the education they need. Kids come starving for that little hug or pat that motivates them. The staff does this. With that little extra, when you motivate a child, it works out good. I think it's mostly the principal that pushes to motivate the kids. She knows it, she shows it, and she shows it by doing. The principal sees that kids get what they need.

And, as we have indicated, the parents shared a similar opinion, adding "problem solver" to the list of key leadership attributes the principal had:

I have never known someone as committed as the principal. She finds solutions instead of finding blame.

Professional Development

Every building in Ridgecrest's school district had a program improvement plan that included participation in districtwide professional development as well as training specific to the school building. Each building also had a staff member whose responsibilities included organizing and facilitating this training. The difference at Ridgecrest, according to the person on its staff who handled this task, was:

Here, I can do my job. We have a set time to do professional development. I'm allowed to do my job with that. I don't do the administrators' work, like others in other buildings do. The amount of work we get done is amazing.

School-based professional development was nearly unavoidable. For example, in the middle of her third year at the school, a teacher had received the efficacy training that served as a cornerstone of the approach that the principal expected all members of the school community to use with one another, an optional series of workshops on how to address student diversity in the classroom, and year-long training in a literacy program that would eventually be introduced at all grades.

Professional development was built into the schedule for the teams being trained in a particular topic. For example, teachers in one training effort met every Wednesday at 11:30 A.M. In addition, the teachers at each grade level met nearly every day, using a common lunch period. The conversations, according to a kindergarten teacher, revolved around particular children's needs as well as curriculum.

The teacher went on to describe how they meshed the reading curriculum with students' reading levels—and with the school's commitment to avoid grouping students for reading:

> Ridgecrest is in the minority [in the district] by not regrouping students for reading instruction. We believe deeply in the "efficacy" model and are opposed to sorting and labeling. What we do is work to differentiate instruction to meet the different needs. We follow the Patricia Cunningham model with four blocks for reading:
>
> (1) Guided reading. We already had this in place. It is usually done as a whole-class activity, with everyone reading the same thing.
>
> (2) Writers workshop. This is multilevel [kids working at their own level] and often done one-on-one.
>
> (3) Word works. This is done with the whole class, with everyone working on the same assignment. We had some of this in place already.
>
> (4) Readers workshop. We didn't have this before. It is basically self-selected reading, so it is very multilevel, with lots of conferencing one-on-one.
>
> The premise is that all children can read and write and that kids learn in different ways. It all seemed like a beautiful fit for our school.

Opportunities were made available to parents as well. One kindergarten teacher reported that parents of 9 of the 23 children in the class took part in the literacy training. The effect was that parents became more in tune with what the school was trying to do and more cognizant of how it was going about pursuing those ends.

The perennial problem for parents with such an approach is that while they may value diversity in the classroom, they do not want the wide range of performance levels to hold their particular children back. One of the participating parents offered this commentary on how one of the training efforts open to parents altered her thinking in this respect:

> I went to the efficacy training class. My thing is you can always learn something. There, I realized that they didn't do any grouping here because kids become labeled. Now, last year in kindergarten, there was a boy who was having problems. It made me wonder about having everyone in the same class. But I tried to make this experience positive for my son. I explained that the other child was just different. Eventually I had a chance to meet the child's mother and I understood what was going on. So there are pros and cons, but I see that it is positive for kids. Positive peer pressure can help.

Education Assistants

Ridgecrest was a magnet school. Traditionally the school's approach required the presence of education assistants in each classroom. The principal had been able to maintain a nearly full complement of such people, despite an overall trend in the district to reduce the number of classroom aides. This continuity had led people to think of each classroom as having two teachers. In fact, on a bulletin board in the school's lobby, each pair's photograph appeared along with their grade assignment; there was no designation made as to who was the teacher and who was the assistant. Two of the assistants described their position this way, highlighting the availability of extra help for children who needed it:

> My most important work is working one-on-one with students or with a couple of them. The teacher does the lesson and the students who have focusing issues, I can sit with them and give them extra help.

> Since one person can't be everywhere, I can help. There is not enough time for the teacher to spend with everyone. The teacher needs help. Some children just need someone to sit next to them.

We asked one of the assistants to describe how she worked with her teacher.

She responded, "I work the classroom. The importance of my job is not singling out students who may be struggling but helping to bring them along."

"Can you give me an example?"

"Today, Moni was having trouble with her work. I went over to give her some extra assistance and when I knew she understood it, I gave the teacher the high sign so she could call on her and she would be successful. There are some students who just need that kind of positive reinforcement. I'm in the classroom so that if the students don't get it the way the teacher explains it, I can do it another way. It's also important that I am there all day so I can see the continuity and the structure."

"How do the students respond to you?"

"The kids see me as a second teacher. I am very fortunate. I work with a good teacher. We work closely together. We are always talking about alternative strategies to reach the kids. It is best when the kids get very frustrated, when they don't get something, and the teacher must move on. I am there to help them."

"So, do you ever pull kids out of class for special help?"

"If I pull them out, they feel it. Then they won't ask for help. But if they don't feel singled out, they'll ask for help. We were working on the concept of 'greater than' in math. Everyone in the class got it except one boy. I just sat down with him and used an illustration. We cut up a candy bar into two unequal parts. It only took 2 minutes and he got it."

"Do you think that most of the assistants work this way with their teachers?"

"I would say about 75% have the same experience. But the principal is working toward making it 100%."

"How is she doing this?"

"She observes the classes constantly to make sure we are working with the students. She is open to our concerns. For example, she doesn't want to see us as clerks at the copy machine all the time. She has an open-door policy."

"Why does Ridgecrest have so many assistants when others in the district don't?"

"The principal fights hard to keep them. Our test scores prove that it works. We also know how the students do when they walk away from here."

"So you feel valued here?"

"We are respected and not looked down upon. The principal leads the way on this. The kids don't slip through the cracks because we have two people to watch the quiet strugglers. We just see it, and we don't even have to discuss it."

"Any idea what parents think about assistants?"

"That is a lot of the reason they come to Ridgecrest, because of the 'second teacher' role."

Another assistant gave us an idea of what her day looked like. In doing so, the person made it clear why others in the people had begun to look upon the assistants as "second" teachers. Their assumption of responsibility for student learning mirrored that of the teachers, which in turn engendered reciprocated respect for the assistants:

> Most of us do the same kinds of things. We usually start early, like 30 to 45 minutes before the students get here. I sit down with [the teacher] and we go over the schedule. Sometimes we may try and point out which kids I will probably need to sit with. We also check over homework in the morning. During class I walk around and make sure that they are all working. I also take kids to and from specials. Basically my job is working with the kids. I have worked with [the teacher] for so long we read each other's minds. We can just look at each other and know what to do. The students see me as a equal to the teacher because she treats me as an equal. The kids are just as likely to come to me for help. That is just the way we are in this program. People are overwhelmed that everyone gets along so well. In the other schools the aides aren't with children constantly like we are, because the Bank Street program requires it. At summer school our peers can't believe what we do. The teachers in the other schools don't know what we do.

Having the assistants available to work with students was a feature of the school that was very attractive to parents:

> That's great. It is an added touch to the school. I had not seen this in the other schools. You have a class ratio that is already great and then there is an extra adult. You've got that buffer for when a child woke up and is having a bad day.

After hearing the principal, teachers, parents, students, and assistants describe how crucial the position was to supporting children's education, we began informally and nonscientifically polling teachers in our other projects about whether they would prefer smaller classes or classes of the same size with an assistant. Responses were mixed outside Ridgecrest, with a bias toward smaller classes. People expressed concern about the "quality" of the assistants and the difficulty in getting people who were "competent." This was not a concern at Ridgecrest, as the above comments attested.

Moreover, the principal made a commitment to offer the assistants training opportunities similar to what the teachers received. For example, in the last year of our study, the school's focus was on special-needs students, and so the assistants explored the topic of learning disabilities. During the fall, they participated in three sessions, each with an expert. These sessions occurred during the schoolday, on school time, because, as the principal explained, "They are so underpaid to ask them to come on their own time. Besides, they will also know how valued they are."

The assistants were aware of their special status in the building:

> We will have assistants' meeting districtwide. There is never a complaint from our school about our role. We're here for the children. If we are not doing something in our job description and it is helping children, we don't care.

School-Based Standards

As noted much earlier in this chapter, the school was beginning an attempt to define performance standards for students at each grade. A number of the comments on student expectations, especially those that reflected an attempt to establish absolute expectations, probably were both stimuli for and products of the emphasis on standards in the school. These standards were specific to the school, in support of but distinct from those established in Ridgecrest's district and state. We found that most of the teachers had already set standards personally. The second-grade teacher quoted at the beginning of this case was just one example. Other teachers described their thoughts about standards, emphasizing the need to prepare all students to cope well with the "real world":

> We want kids to do well. The world is very demanding. You've got to be prepared for it. Success is getting whatever you want out of life. Kids need to be prepared. We don't want them to fail, so we look at where they need to be.

We mentioned the "standards movement" within the school earlier. One of the teachers in the fifth grade had added a couple to the ones the entire grade had agreed upon:

Our school is instituting standards. All kids have to reach them to attend promotion. I chose some others for my kids also, like being able to do math in their heads. Even if they are learning-disabled, I don't want them using their fingers. I also was pushing for more writing being included.

The principal referred to the fifth grade as "the [school's] vanguard for the standards movement."

We wanted benchmarks for our leaving fifth-graders, to show they were successful. That was wonderful. Now, we are working backwards, coupling two grades together. So the fifth-grade standards have elevated the other grades.

IN REACH OF EXCELLENCE

The principal politely but firmly refused our requests to use standardized test scores in writing this case study. The disaggregated scores showed remarkable progress in closing the achievement gap. The problem was that the job was not complete, according to the principal, and she wanted no one to feel as if this progress signaled that it was. Besides, the principal added, with the student groups (such as low-income, African American males) who traditionally had not done well in school, "I know by the way they speak, act, and dress that they are not uptight about school."

Others in the district regarded Ridgecrest's success as not necessarily replicable elsewhere. After all, they claimed, it was a magnet school, which meant that it may have attracted an atypical student population. On this count, they were partially right. The school had slightly fewer students who were eligible for free and reduced-price lunches than the average elementary school in the city, but, on the other hand, it had a distinctly larger special education population.

The factor that other educators in the district most envied was the high parent participation in school activities. They seemed to regard this as the school's greatest advantage over the other schools. This was ironic, especially because Ridgecrest's faculty maintained so strongly that they viewed this participation as enriching a child's education but not as securing the child's education. Promoting student academic success was the school's responsibility regardless of the role parents played.

If the customer is always right, then Ridgecrest's parents offered the most meaningful commentary that the school was moving in the right direction. The parents took great pride in the school's public achievements and often touted what that progress had to say about the school's quality. But what really mattered to the parents was the progress of their own children, and perhaps that is the best evidence for the school's effectiveness. Four commented on their children:

> My son has special needs—some neurological damage from being premature. He has surpassed everyone's expectations. They really take an interest in each individual child.

> My son is really being challenged.

> My kids [first and fifth grades] learn with enthusiasm. They want to read and do math. They want me to do math charts with them. When they are home, they show that enthusiasm. You can fill that up with a whole lot of good stuff.

> Ridgecrest brings kids and parents to school to achieve academic success.

The principal relayed perhaps a signature story about the school's influence on students who had not traditionally done well. One particular student had struggled considerably in a class but also had been striving to do his work. Still, the effort had left him on the borderline between a B and a C. The teacher told the child that she was going to give him the benefit of the doubt and that she would allow him to squiggle just over into B territory, due to this effort. The student went home and told his mother about this conversation and told her that he did not feel like he deserved the B yet. He wanted the teacher to give him the grade he felt he deserved, which was the C. Beaming with pride, the principal noted: "This speaks powerfully to our efficacy model and the environment we are trying to create here."

7

The Meaning of an "It's My Job" Belief

Just as the previous three chapters were essentially one extremely long, continuous segment of this book, so too are these final chapters. Chapters 4–6 peered into classrooms and schools where the performance of low-income students reflected both effort and excellence; Chapters 7 and 8 serve as a "discussion" of those data-filled sections. The first of these two concluding chapters extrapolates what we feel are the most salient points to note at the classroom level, while the final one delves into the infrastructure that is needed to support teachers' assuming the responsibility for all children's succeeding.

We do not intend for educators and schools hoping to close the achievement gap between low- and high-performing students to emulate Edna, Craig, Margaret, Jim, Granite, and Ridgecrest as models. To be sure, each took actions and developed ideas worthy of consideration. But we have been in many classrooms where teachers had students work in groups, where teachers tried to connect classroom content to students' lives outside school, where teachers engaged the different learning styles of their students, where teachers offered to give additional help to struggling students, and where teachers called the homes of poorly performing or behaving students. We have been in many schools that established ways of providing extra help to their students, that established rubrics defining levels of quality for student work, that altered traditional forms of grading students, that increased the opportunities for teachers to work together, and that emphasized professional development. One can find numerous references to all of these steps in the literature on working with low-performing students.

However, if these lists of "best practices" were truly powerful and effective, then we should not be seeing the stark and frightening disparities in achievement that currently exist. Something else must be missing in the abundant push to adopt "whole-school" models of reform. We think that it is the belief system. We have seen how "All children can succeed" is an umbrella that accommodates multiple meanings, most of which establish limits to what schools can do to ensure success for all. Only the "It's my job"/"No excuses" approach refuses to accept such limits. And this "approach" is simply a belief that educators must do anything and everything to see to it that every last child achieves at a high level.

More and more, the educational world is recognizing and accepting that the proof of reform is in the classroom. Three well-known statements of this position come quickly to mind. The first is the evaluation of Philadelphia's $150-million, 5-year Children Achieving initiative. Conducted by the Consortium for Policy Research in Education (CPRE), this evaluation concentrated on three basic questions: Were the reforms being carried out as envisioned? Were the instructional practices of teachers and the learning experiences of students changing in ways that would improve outcomes? And could improvements be attributed to these reforms? CPRE invested much of its time assembling classroom data—through observations, interviews, and surveys—as the best means for determining the true impact of this reform (CPRE, 1997). The effort was noteworthy as one of the first evaluations of large-scale urban reform to so intensively build directly gathered information about classroom life into its design.

A second example is the publication of *The Black–White Test Score Gap* (Jencks & Phillips, 1998), in which the authors examine the persistent gap in performance between African American and Caucasian students. They argue convincingly, and at considerable length, that it is much more productive to pay attention to students' classroom experiences than to genetics, poverty, or ethnicity as explanations for the disparity.

The third example carries the argument one step further. Deschenes, Tyack, and Cuban (2001) review the ways in which schools have located the source of the problem with students who traditionally have not meet educators' academic expectations. Rather than emphasizing deficits in students and/or their families, these authors stress that not only should educators consider what goes on in school as a primary explanation for student failure but also they should thoughtfully and thoroughly adapt school practices to resolve the mismatch between some students and school.

On the one hand, the obvious reaction should be "So what else is new?" On the other hand, this burgeoning idea is profound. We can build the most lavish and technically advanced ship in the world, but if we cannot steer it effectively, then all those resources become tragically wasted. Similarly, we can propose, fund, and implement many changes in our educational system, but if the classroom remains a place of inequitable distribution of opportunities to learn, then the changes will have been for naught. We are arguing therefore that any adopted practices and policies have to become infused with the belief that the success of students is solely in the hands of educators.

We understand that it is a scary prospect for educators to take on this responsibility. So the major portion of this section is devoted to a closer look at what "It's my job" in the classroom looks and sounds like. The following examples come from settings in which the teachers, students, and observations all suggested that a belief in the responsibility of educators to ensure success prevailed. These classrooms, like those of the four teachers profiled in Chapter 4, operated in sharp contrast to those elsewhere in their respective buildings, according to students. Only at Granite and Ridgecrest did teachers have the benefit of schoolwide expectations and support for their assuming the responsibility for all children's succeeding.

To an extent, what follows is an attempt to categorize some of the actions described earlier—that is, to extract common actions and attitudes. However, there is a danger in doing this, and that is that these actions and attitudes will be viewed as recommendations, or even principles to follow. This is far from what we hope to do. We simply wish to enrich the concept of "closing the gap" by offering a myriad of examples of how a potentially constructive belief system becomes manifested in the classroom. Our goal is to make this approach more familiar and thus appear possible.

Finally, the following discussion is in no way an effort to identify "effective instructional practices." These are well known, although not always implemented. Most teachers know about varying instructional activities to accommodate different learning styles, using cooperative groups with individual accountability, tapping the multiple intelligences of their students, connecting classroom content to students' everyday lives, and establishing an atmosphere of respect for others and oneself in the classroom.

The teachers at Granite and Ridgecrest as well as Edna, Craig, Margaret, and Jim relied on these practices. So, too, did many other teachers in the schools we studied. Thus using good instructional practice does not separate the "It's my job"/"No excuses" teachers from the others. Adhering to the belief that teachers are responsible for student success does.

Of course, we would be foolish to lump everything good and true and beautiful under the label of "It's my job." Remember that we started this book by stating that we were only looking for insights about enabling all children to succeed from the large group of people who already espoused the belief that success for all was achievable. It was the distinctions that those within that group made about the conditions under which such success was realizable that led us to recognizing the significance of teachers who accepted full responsibility for student success. Many of the teachers we saw used what would be termed "effective" practice. They were creative, entertaining, rigorous, consistent, and caring. But not all students seemed to succeed in creative, entertaining, rigorous, consistent, and caring teachers' classrooms, as long as the responsibility for success remain lodged, at least partially, with students and/or their parents.

We therefore offer the following discussion as "supportive actions" in enacting the belief that it is the responsibility of the teacher and the school to create the conditions in which all students succeed. It contains examples not so much of good instruction but of good instructors who shouldered the additional burden of ensuring their students' success. So do not look here for reinforcement for implementing varied instruction, using groups, connecting to students' lives, and the like. Look here for ways that teachers actually took seriously the word *all* in "All children can succeed" and ignored the reasons why that word is for so many only an ideal.

In this chapter, we also occasionally bring in more data from our study. We know that a reader will have gotten the gist of the actions discussed below from the prior chapters, but we think these points will come to life better with a few additional examples.

CLASSROOM MANIFESTATIONS OF TEACHERS' BEING RESPONSIBLE FOR STUDENT LEARNING

Enacting one's responsibility for all students' making an effort and demonstrating excellence cannot be done via a simple checklist. But we do not mean that the concept must remain vague and totally elusive either. Quite the contrary. We encountered a number of situations in which teachers both verbalized such beliefs and demonstrated ways to bring them to action. This next section spells out four of these ways.

Insisting That Students Complete Every Assignment

In our minds, this action probably is most central to putting an "It's my job" philosophy into motion and may be the most powerful mechanism by which this philosophy leads to closing the achievement gap. Put simply, if an assignment is worth doing, it is worth completing.

Each assignment is, in fact, a bridge that connects prior learning to new learning. Crossing this bridge precludes a student from having to devise his or her own means of making progress, especially ones that may be carried out without professional assistance and divorced from the context in which the assignment was given—such as making up an assignment at the end of a marking period. Completing each assignment should be viewed as paving the way for success on subsequent assignments. On the other hand, allowing incomplete assignments or accepting assignments that have been completed poorly (another action addressed below) creates diversions on the path to high achievement. The less work students do and the more work they do poorly, the more they will stray farther from that goal.

We are biased, of course, but we think that this action is a theme that flashes in neon in Chapters 4–6. The teachers talked about "staying on students" to do their work and "keeping track" of who had done what. However, instead of recording zeros for unfinished work, the teachers continued their hounding. They created other times during the day when the students would have to catch up—during recess or after school. Assignment completion, in fact, served as the operating principle for Granite Junior High. The salient point, though, is that the teachers and the school saw it as their responsibility to ensure that all students completed every task.

The consequence for students of not finishing their work was having to spend more time on the assignment, not the reprieve offered by a bad grade. Schools and teachers did not leave it to students to find such time on their own. Instead, according to students, they had to pass up going to free time after lunch or morning breaks or special classes or, sometimes, home until they finished. In each case, however, a teacher was available to help explain the assignment and to provide extra help, which is a critical aspect of "It's my job." Rarely were students left without guidance to do a crucial learning activity.

Students did not necessarily perceive having to make up assignments as punishment. Frankly, nearly every student we talked to preferred that teachers insist on assignment completion and accepted that they would have to miss some other, potentially more attractive, parts of the schoolday to do this. They viewed it as determining whether they learned or not. Repeatedly, students justified a teacher's incessant badgering as focused on learning.

The preference cut across grade levels, refusing to fade even as students moved to the age where most people might say "It's time they did their work for themselves." As we saw, Craig's and Margaret's students, as well as those at Granite Junior High, clearly showed that an

"It's my job" teacher was a valued teacher. A common phrase was that the teacher did not "leave us on our own."

A common complaint of teachers who worked with students who traditionally had not done well in school was that they devoted too much energy to discipline, leaving a shortage of time that could be spent on instruction. This created a huge dilemma for teachers insistent on students' completing their assignments. As Jim noted earlier, during his first year he sent unruly students to the office so that they would not disturb others. However, in the second year, after realizing that "all" students probably should include even the unruly, he altered his approach so that the focus was on instruction rather than on discipline.

We experienced an example of enabling instruction to remain the classroom focus in the face of misbehavior during a middle school science lesson.

> *A student was working on a small-group task with fellow eighth-graders who were unraveling the mystery of the structure of the atom. The young man in question was not a "strong" student. His usual strategy, according to the teacher, when confronted with challenging work was to tune out, often dragging others along with him.*
>
> *The teacher began the class with an invitation from the boy's group to help him out. When she got to them, she found the student talking with a neighbor. Rather than chastising him, the teacher simply said: "[student's name], you are going to have to pay attention now because this next question is yours." She then asked him how many neutrons there were in a particular element and what the mass number was. He answered correctly.*
>
> *The teacher explained that there was a general formula for arriving at this calculation and asked this same student to help her construct that formula (i.e., mass − protons = neutrons). She guided the group through an example with real numbers and then said: "Now let's see if you really understand this." She went to the board and portrayed the mass number as a smiley face (drawing a picture) and the number of protons as a sad face. She handed the chalk to the student who had not been paying attention originally and had him write the formula on the board. He did it correctly.*
>
> *The teacher then said: "Let's check for level of understanding. Hands up for those who follow this?" (All hands quickly went up.) She replied: "Super job!"*

The teacher's skill in bringing the whole class toward a better understanding did not go unnoticed by her students:

> INTERVIEWER: Why did the whole class begin listening to the teacher when she only started explaining it to a small group?
> STUDENT: The students want to get their work done right, and they know they will have it right when they listen to her.

This example, and the others like it in the previous chapters, are intended to show that assignment completion served as a guiding principle for life in certain teachers' classrooms. Everything that happened in those rooms had implications for whether work was being completed or not, and the teacher brought this point home time and time again. Recess, disruptive behavior, failure to do well in school in prior years—they all were subordinate to whether or not a student had done an assignment and, as is discussed next, done it well.

Expecting Students to Do High-Quality Work

As we mentioned in the last chapter, Lipman (1998) describes the pitfalls of rewarding low-achieving students for effort rather than high-quality work. To be sure, "making an effort" is an important step for students to take on the way to success, but to close the achievement gap, the "It's my job" educators argued that the effort had to result in completed work of acceptable quality. This approach then meshes well with the standards movement in this country. Work must be done to a certain standard; if that standard is not met, then the work must be redone until it is met.

We saw this emphasis throughout the earlier examples. For Edna, nothing less than a C was acceptable. At Granite, students had to get a B or they kept working. Usually, it seemed that teachers had sufficiently established rubrics for what B work would look like that it was reasonably clear to everyone whether a certain piece of work had attained that standard. The ninth grade was an exception to this rule at Granite. There the teachers found it important to begin preparing students for the failure-inclusive grading system in place at the high school. Margaret, as we heard, was extremely agitated over the willingness of her high school peers to accept sloppy work and to hold lowered expectations for what students in the school could accomplish, so she would have preferred Granite's influence to trickle up rather than having the traditional grading practices at the high school trickle down.

We met numerous teachers in this study, particularly at the secondary level, who maintained that they had high, unyielding standards. Often the proof of these standards, they said, was the low grades of their students. No contributors to grade inflation they. The salient difference between holding high standards and being an "It's my job"/ "No excuses" teacher with high standards was that the latter created an environment in which those standards were actually achieved.

This message was something that teachers who assumed responsibility for engendering effort and excellence communicated regularly in their classrooms. An illustration of the importance that these teachers placed on doing quality work occurred in this brief exchange in a second-grade classroom during a science experiment. Although students tended to view the activity as fun, they discovered that doing things well still played a role.

There was a great deal of excitement and anticipation as the students awaited cutting open a sample fruit or vegetable of their own choosing. They were supposed to assess the number of seeds on the inside—about which they had already made a guess. Prior to this step, though, the teacher had instructed the class that they had to first draw an acceptable representation of the exterior of their plant. Since the teacher was wielding the knife that would cut open each specimen, he was able to evaluate whether the drawings were acceptable, prior to the dissection step. The students naturally wanted to move quickly to counting the seeds on the inside of the fruit or vegetable, but the teacher did not permit that until he saw a satisfactory drawing.

One pair of students in particular really struggled with their diagram of an apple. The student who worked on the drawing was fussy and made several aborted attempts. She grew frustrated and was on the verge of quitting. The teacher walked over and inspected her last attempt to draw the apple. He concurred that the representation was not acceptable, but rather than leave her to founder, he suggested that she trace the fruit. He bent over the page and helped the student guide her pencil around the apple. With some minor adjustments, she finally arrived at a representation that satisfied both. He congratulated her: "You're done!" She finally smiled, and she and her partner eagerly watched as the teacher cut the apple in two, exposing the seeds they could now finally count.

Middle school teachers also paired standards with making sure that the standards were attained. In one science classroom we visited, the teacher displayed "Are you caught up?" charts on the walls, much as Jim Evans had done. In this instance, students could not conduct certain experiments until they had finished a particular unit of work. Consequently, at any one time in the class, an observer would find students working on different topics and activities. This was not the norm in this school, but rather something the teacher himself believed was important:

> I work on a mastery system in here. The kids know exactly what they have to do to get an A, B, or C. Anything below that is really an incomplete.

When students talked about the value of this approach in their interviews, they introduced an important element into their language. Instead of simply referring to the importance of doing work, as we had heard in another of our studies on low-income classrooms (Wilson & Corbett, 2001), these students talked about knowledge as the reason for completing one's work. Completion, then, was a means to an end, not the end itself. As one student noted:

> You can move at your own rate. You get a better education that way. You can move on when you *know* how to do it. You can learn more that way.

A student with another "It's my job"–type teacher responded similarly:

> INTERVIEWER: You said your teacher keeps after you to do your work right. Do you like this?
> STUDENT: Yes! If not, I wouldn't be passing. I just wouldn't *know* the things I *know*. Some teachers just tell you to do the work without any hints. But this teacher is one I can get help from.

Teachers emphasized that it was important for students to understand what "quality" work was. Thus their classrooms seemed to be filled with feedback about students' work as a means of reaching that shared definition. This was often done publicly to increase the chance that all students in the class were getting the same message, as the following field notes detail:

> *The teacher begins her feedback to a student who reported on the development of space stations by summarizing his strengths (e.g., strong introduction, nice structure to the presentation, and*

*the introduction of a game as a wonderful recap of the key points),
but she also offers very direct and helpful criticisms: "You need
to make sure you know your visuals well" (he stumbled several
times when presenting them) and "you need to reduce the number of times you use the words* and, like, *and* they. *In fact, I want
to address the whole class about this. I guess I will just have to
get a can with rocks in it and shake it every time I hear you use
those words."*

*She then turns to a special education teacher who also mod-
els the same behavior by highlighting several strengths and some
areas where he could improve: "You should check the pronuncia-
tion of several words and the distraction to the audience as you
fumble with your note cards."*

*Finally, the teacher also uses a teacher intern as yet a third
critic with his suggestions: "The fluidity of the presentation needs
more practice, and more creativity could be introduced by making use of the visuals you have on display."*

*In addition to this on-the-spot feedback from adults, the
classroom teacher also incorporates some student feedback. At
the beginning of the class session, she passes out a worksheet for
each "observer" in the class to complete, having defined "observer" as a role all students listening to the exhibition presenter
are to play. The students are to think of five questions they want
answered about the topic, and they write these down and check
whether the presenter answers them during the presentation. In
addition, the observers are asked to write responses to two other
questions: "What did you like best about the presentation?" and
"I would like to still learn more about [the exhibition]." These
"evaluations" are collected at the end of the class period as the
students' tickets out the door to lunch. These evaluations are
passed along to the presenters as another tool to assist them in
refining and improving their exhibitions.*

A student's reaction to the experience reflected clearly the teacher's belief that producing quality work required making a continual
effort to polish it:

INTERVIEWER: Did you learn much from your exhibition?
STUDENT: Yes.
INTERVIEWER: Like what?
STUDENT: I have learned how to take notes, how to summarize in-

formation, how to display visuals, and how to do research
  for high school.
INTERVIEWER: Do you think it prepares you well for high school?
STUDENT: Yes.
INTERVIEWER: Why?
STUDENT: You and your exhibition become one, and each
  teaches the other. You also learn to think a lot!

In a succinct closing to a lesson, one secondary teacher illustrated
the inseparable connection between completing one's work and completing it well:

> I want to collect your worksheets, but please don't turn them in
> unless it is quality work.

There was no "turn in what you have," no partial credit offered. "Do
it and do it well," was the teacher's message, "and only then are you
done."

Checking for All Students' Understanding

In one of our other studies of inner-city students, as well as in most of
the student interviews we conducted in the two school districts, we
found that students value a consistent set of instruction-related qualities in teachers—willing to help, strict (and, if possible, nice), and able
to explain the work clearly (Corbett & Wilson, 1998; Wilson & Corbett,
2001). One indicator of these traits was how thoroughly a teacher
checked with each student to see if he or she, in fact, understood what
they were to do. This checking then determined the extent to which
the teacher needed to arrange for extra help for several students, repeat
explanations for the entire class, or provide different explanations for
the same assignment.
  Thus one means of shouldering the responsibility for student
learning was diligently making sure that the entire class grasped the
work. Perhaps the most striking illustration of the multiple strategies
teachers used to do this occurred in a middle school social studies
classroom. There, in the course of a few short minutes, we observed a
host of little actions that seemed to heighten students' attention and
understanding.

> *The class in question had been reading a passage about colonial
> trade. One teacher directed the lesson, while the other floated*

around the room to answer questions. Both teachers used questions about the information to make sure students were following along with the passage—for example, "Who issued the Proclamation of 1763?" and "Who had more power, the parliament or the king?" The teachers divided the class into teams, and each team member had a number. The teachers held a big spinner with two dials at the front of the class. One spinning dial represented a team number and the other, a member within the team. Students were always expected to be ready with an answer.

Along the way, the teachers frequently posited analogies between the material and students' lives. In one instance, describing the relationship between the colonists and England, one teacher offered, "It was kind of like a parent telling a teenager that no one could come over to the house to visit while the parent was not home."

There were also frequent, gentle, but insistent reminders to students about the importance of their completing their work. The teachers reminded students to try and visualize what they were reading, asking "What does it look like?" and "What does it sound like?"

With the students in groups, the teachers continually pointed out the presence of the extra resources around them: "I want you to talk to your partner and have the two of you figure it out. I want you to get the big picture on this one. What was the Act designed to do?"

Finally, every 5 or 10 minutes they briefly conferred with one another privately, checking to see if they both concurred about whether students understood both their instructions and the content they were trying to convey. They referred to their approach as a "tag-team effort."

In principle, most teachers would agree with the value of making sure that everyone understands an assignment. We found it common, however, for teachers to check with just a few students and to assume that this sample's understanding was representative of the class, or to ask a student if he or she understood and then settle for a head nod rather than a restatement of what that understanding was.

The implications for a student who did not want to stand out by admitting a lack of understanding occurred in an example from a fifth-grade mathematics lesson.

As part of the lesson, students were working either individually or in pairs, using "Reversa Tile" boards to match sets of tiles into patterns based on computations. The problems they were solving involved addition of fractions. The teacher turned the class loose to work on their own. Most of the individuals or pairs whizzed through the assignment. Several had even begun a second set of problems (with 24 in each set).

A quiet youngster, working on his own, clearly struggled with the work but did not solicit the teacher's help. He tried valiantly to work the problems out for himself. While everyone else was on the second set of problems, he was still working with the ninth problem of the first set of 24. He had to add $\frac{5}{8}$ and $\frac{1}{8}$. The answer he came up with was $\frac{6}{8}$, but that was not an available answer among the ones from which he could choose. The worksheet only listed $\frac{3}{4}$. He had not thought of reducing the number to its lowest terms.

The teacher eventually walked by and asked if he was "okay." He said "yes." She continued on. Finally she came around a second time; recognizing that he was still on the same problem, she asked if he was stuck. He admitted that he was, and she quickly saw his problem and told him he needed to reduce the fraction. He understood what to do and found the correct answer of $\frac{3}{4}$ among the choices.

The teacher moved on. He added the next pair of fractions. This one was more complicated, since there was no common denominator. He was completely stumped, again. The teacher, again, asked if he needed help. He said "no." She went off to help others.

He sat there puzzled for several more minutes. Finally, as everyone packed up, the teacher suggested that he concentrate more on his homework. She said that if he had more problems that he should get a note and come see her (during his other classes or after school).

It was entirely possible that, later, the student received the necessary help. The point, though, is that a cursory checking for understanding via head nods or volunteered hands placed the responsibility for acknowledging confusion on the student. The "It's my job" educators we talked with never assumed that that responsibility would be accepted.

We turn again to students to underline the value of a teacher's taking the time to see if everyone is ready to move on or not. Popping up continuously in quotes similar to the following was the word *different*. Their teachers possessed and shared with students multiple explanations and were willing to exhaust and then extend their instructional bag of tricks until all students nodded in understanding:

> He stops everything and explains it. He keeps trying something *different* until you understand it.

> He tries to include everybody. Like, if you are not paying attention, you know he is going to call on you. But he won't embarrass you. If you can't answer him, he will ask it in a *different* way.

> INTERVIEWER: What does your teacher do if you don't understand?
> STUDENT: He gives us examples. He always has examples. Like today, everyone needed an example [of a data chart]. He also has us come in after school.
> INTERVIEWER: What does he do?
> STUDENT: He puts it in a way so everyone understands. He puts it in a *different* way—so that we are both laughing and learning.

Providing Extra Help

An inevitable consequence of educating humans is that they all will tend to acquire, process, and retain what they learn in different ways and at different speeds. While all educators are now likely aware of and accept the truth of this situation, the structure of most schools would lead one to assume that the opposite is the case. Grade levels, 45-minute class periods, and timed assessments reinforce the notion that learning "on time" outweighs the importance of learning "eventually."

Certain teachers and schools, however, put themselves in the position of having to think smartly about time if they were going to fulfill their expectation that it is up to them for every child to try and do well in school. As they insisted that everyone understand what they were to do, complete the assignment, and do it well, the teachers ran head on into the varying rates at which their students accomplished these things. One alternative for them was to accept the developmental and readiness differences among students and to devise individual goals; another was to create situations in which extra help was available to those students who needed it. The former, it seemed to teachers, contained the danger of accepting the inevitability of a performance gap. That is, although altering the standards certain children were expected to meet would make it possible for all children to succeed, it would also perpetuate differences in their learning levels. The latter, on the other hand, necessitated a lot of work on the teachers' and school's part.

Individual teachers, therefore, have to be—quite frankly—superpeople. Edna, Margaret, Jim, and Craig came early to school and often stayed late, belying the fact that they had lives outside their occupations. They also developed lessons that afforded them the opportunity to visit with individuals. Essentially they took advantage of any "downtime" in the existing schedule to work with needy students. The teachers at Granite and Ridgecrest had an advantage in that the schools scheduled time for additional help and they received continual administrative praise for finding informal opportunities. Also, both schools put an additional adult in the classrooms to give assistance—during the blocked class periods at Granite and via the education assistants at Ridgecrest.

Thus the schools and teachers recognized that providing extra help to low-performing students was an inescapable fact of life in low-income schools. Current policy initiatives to reduce class size, to increase the number of adults in the classroom (through either education assistants or volunteers), and to create after-school programs are avenues for offering the kind of extra help that children who traditionally have not performed well in school will need to begin to catch up to their counterparts.

PROMOTING EFFORT AND EXCELLENCE
IN LOW-INCOME CLASSROOMS

If schoolwork is worth doing, then all children need to do it *and* do it well. That was a principle by which certain teachers we studied lived by in their classrooms. Their fear was that settling solely for increased effort would shortchange the students. For them, effort plus excellence equaled true success.

Because children bring diverse backgrounds and preparation to these tasks, schools must be organized so that students get all the necessary help they need to do these tasks well at school. Otherwise, the diversity in students' home situations will inevitably reflect itself in their performance. Thus, when teachers adopted an "It's my job" perspective, they acknowledged that they would be spending a great deal of time supplying extra help to their students.

There are numerous means by which schools and teachers can arrange for such help. Earlier, we referred to some of these: using normal schoolday breaks, being available before and after school, having another adult around to work with students, and so forth. If the belief that there is no reason why every student cannot succeed at this work permeates the institution, then any and all of these will be used.

The teachers depicted in Chapter 4 and the schools in Chapters 5 and 6 did not necessarily follow a common formula for achieving the results that they did. Certainly they pushed students constantly to do their assignments. They insisted that students do this with quality. They continually checked to see whether students understood what they were doing. And they arranged for assistance whenever the student required it. These actions were carried out in the fervent hope that they would catch any students in danger of failing. The actions were cords in the safety net the educators were constructing within their schools. If these proved weak, then they would seek other means of securing children's education. Assuming responsibility for student success, therefore, was a way of asserting that "schools can make a difference" for students—for all students—even in the absence of parental support and prior student motivation.

But the common denominator was as much their attitude as their actions. "No excuses" and "It's my job" meant, quite simply, doing whatever it took to get the job done. If what teachers were doing did not work, then they did not declare the task of raising the performance of some students to be impractical. Neither did they claim that small groups, hands-on lessons, and rubrics were ineffective and impractical. They did not try to place blame or to find excuses for student failure. They looked for solutions.

8

Becoming a School Where All Children Can Succeed

One of the positive developments that has grown out of the recent, nearly obsessive attention devoted to accountability has been an increased concern with the achievement differences among various groups of students (Haycock, 2001). While our work has called attention to the persistent gap between poorer and wealthier students, much of the popular and academic literature has focused on the achievement gap between Caucasian and Hispanic or African American students (e.g., Hoff, 2000). In 2000 and 2001 alone, this topic was the focus of 223 commentaries, editorials, or in-depth reports in the 50 most widely read newspapers in the country. A sampling of these included the following:

- *A New York Times* editorial ("Fix the Flaws," 2001) about the need to rebuild failing schools in addition to just identifying those that continually produce students with low test scores
- A news report on an effort by Seattle public school administrators to "zap the gap" ("Schools Unveil Effort," 2001) by getting the community involved in identifying and assisting in implementing improvement strategies
- A description of an advocacy group's effort in Boston to use a recently released report by the Council of the Great City Schools to point out that while achievement overall had improved in the city, closing of the racial gap had lagged behind other urban districts ("Study Hits HUB," 2001)
- An in-depth report of how minority parents in suburban Washington, D.C., refused to wait for social scientists or policy makers to intervene, but rather took issues into their own hands to lobby local districts for more programs to close the achievement gap ("Blacks Battle Achievement Gap," 2000).

Predictably, the literature on this issue is growing at a rate commensurate with the political interest in strategies to ameliorate the achievement gap. Such strategies include: (1) using a multipronged approach including detracking, low-cost test-prep classes, individual tutoring, and shifting extracurricular activities to the schoolday rather than after school (Mezzacappa, 2001); (2) developing better state accountability systems (San Miguel, Garza, & Gibbs, 2000; Viadero, 2000); (3) designing better professional development (Harwell, D'Amico, Stein, & Gatti, 2000); (4) altering federal economic policy (Rothstein, 2000); (5) introducing new local accountability policies (McKenzie Group, 1999); (6) reducing the student–teacher ratio on a state level (Molnar, Smith, & Zahorik, 1999) and a school level (Roach, 2001); and (7) increasing college readiness through K–16 collaboration (Navarro & Natalico, 1999).

But it is a rare exception when the literature also looks at the fundamental beliefs of teachers who must enact these various measures. Our argument—or, rather, the argument that the educators described in the previous chapters would make—is that a belief in educators' responsibility to ensure student success must be the underpinning for any strategy to close the gap. Otherwise, someone will deem a child as unreachable and, thus, establish limits for what a school can do. At this point, then, "Most children can succeed" replaces "All children can succeed," thereby allowing excuses to serve as justifications for failure.

What we saw in the four teachers' classrooms and in the two schools really was a celebration of students' strengths rather than weaknesses, an acknowledgment of what students could do rather than what they could not do. Such an emphasis is not novel. Gordon (2000), Ladson-Billings (1994), Nieto (1996), and Williams (1996) have argued for some time about the theoretical and practical power of taking advantage of students' capabilities and existing knowledge. That many teachers, even those who say all children can succeed, do not act on students' strengths is fundamentally grounded in the teachers' lodging the responsibility for making sure that such strengths are developed with students and parents rather than themselves. The students who appeared to be the most successful in overcoming previously poor records in school had teachers and attended schools that were willing to take on the mantle of responsibility when no one else would.

The important message that needs to be emphasized—and not lost among all the details—is that becoming a school like Granite or Ridgecrest requires a fundamental shift in beliefs. This shift will not happen just by finding a set of promising classroom practices and giving teachers the training to use those practices. Instead, it will require a significant investment of time and money to examine teacher beliefs about students, learning, and instruction; build commitment to an agreed-upon set of valued beliefs; and establish a set of structures and processes that consistently reinforce those beliefs with actions in the classroom. All of this will require a long-term commitment to change.

And the amount of change needed is likely to be substantial. Indeed, we did not find that a majority of teachers subscribed to this approach. In large part that scarcity was a function of the constant vigilance and energy required. Taking an "It's my job"/"No excuses" type of approach required teachers to be constantly vigilant. By asserting that all students could do the work they were given and that it was the teacher's responsibility to ensure that students did the work well, teachers found that they had to hold students accountable and not let them off the hook when work was due. In the words of one, they had to be "unwavering nags." Teachers reported that this was tough work. They admitted that it would have been much easier to abdicate their responsibility to the ever-handy scapegoats of student motivation and home environment.

As we stated earlier, many will argue that we are placing an undue burden on teachers. We cannot deny that this approach requires an incredible amount of individual energy. But that individual energy will only fuel small pockets of success for the few students lucky enough to be assigned to such classrooms until more schools and entire districts move in the same direction as the few isolated teachers and buildings we described previously.

For that reason, we want to draw on the Granite and Ridgecrest experiences to speculate about the kind of support that schools and districts will need to provide in order to adequately reinforce the teachers who already assume responsibility for student success and to encourage others to do so. We hope it is clear that a powerful, transforming belief about the teacher's role in student learning existed in some classrooms and schools that enabled students who traditionally had not done well to succeed. But what will it take to make this happen on a larger scale? And what might be done to set in motion a process of change that causes a shift from making excuses for student failure to becoming effective promoters of student success? The remainder of this concluding chapter offers several thoughts on the type of infrastructure teachers might need to support an "It's my job" type of approach.

AVENUES OF SUPPORT FOR "IT'S MY JOB" EDUCATORS

Using Granite and Ridgecrest as starting points, we maintain that there are at least five avenues that school and district officials could follow to ensure that teachers who are willing to assume responsibility for making sure that students learn do not have to travel this route alone: offering systemic professional development, exhibiting visionary leadership, creating congruent organizational structures, connecting to parents, and establishing complementary policies.

None of these should be news to the reader; each appears on a myriad of lists of reform strategies. Nevertheless, they are worth rehashing here for two reasons. First, we think it is likely that a school and/or district needs to follow all these avenues to achieve a cumulative impact on staff. That is, each should reinforce rather than contradict the others. Otherwise mixed messages ensue and people will become confused about how much the organization really values stated goals. Thus each individual avenue is necessary for supporting educators, but only in concert are they probably sufficient. Second, we want to offer some details on what each avenue might look and sound like in order for it to specifically benefit students who have traditionally not done well in school—enough that they might begin to close the achievement gap that so insidiously permeates much of American education.

Therefore, below we explore what we mean by each of these avenues and point to examples, when available from Granite and Ridgecrest, to illustrate the particular way in which educators were supported. We trust this will provide a useful beginning for other schools and districts to think about in honoring and nurturing educators desperately attempting to raise the achievement of traditionally less successful students.

Systemic Professional Development

Successful education reform demands that all educators engage in comprehensive professional development (Darling-Hammond, 1997; Fullan, 1999). Furthermore, research suggests that among the most important elements common to effective teachers in urban schools is the belief that all students can be successful and the importance of communicating this belief to students (Ladson-Billings, 1994). If new beliefs are to become a vital part of a school's or district's culture, professional development must move beyond imparting technical knowledge and skills to developing a shared understanding and common values.

Our investigations at Granite Junior High and Ridgecrest yielded examples of a rich professional development repertoire that included an exploration of beliefs and values. Ridgecrest offered a year-long literacy program as well as efficacy training, described by teachers and the education assistants as central to enacting the principal's expectations that all staff would effectively address student diversity. Because the new information was intended to affect both attitudes and actions, the principal made provision for numerous opportunities for people to talk about these ideas with one another—in common grade-level lunch periods in particular. Granite also arranged for common times to talk and, in addition, made sure that several faculty had become certified to provide staff development on key topics (such as cooperative groups and brain-based learning) so that teachers would have daily access to experts. The point is that at both schools, professional development enabled staff to learn about topics *and* to develop the habits of mind and action to enact what they had learned by ensuring that there was plenty of conversation among the adults, both formally and informally.

Of course, to specifically target low-income and minority students, professional development has to address important content as well. In other words, teachers have to have significant issues to talk about in their conversations and need to be informed by research on those issues. Recent research on effective instruction in low-income settings (Darling-Hammond, 1997; Knapp et al., 1995; Ladson-Billings, 1990) underlines three important content areas for improving teaching and learning: (1) establishing high expectations for all students, (2) achieving cultural congruence in instruction, and (3) deepening teacher knowledge of teaching strategies. The principals in both schools made sure that teachers not only knew that these topics were important to know about but also knew how to translate them into the classroom.

In our minds, such translation occurs best when the content of teachers' professional development becomes woven into curriculum, assessment, staff evaluations, school policy, and so forth. In that way, classroom applications of what teachers learn become an organizational expectation with systemically concrete reminders embedded in school operation—as opposed to what happens so often in staff development, where application becomes an additional task for each individual teacher to figure out. Thus effective professional development must affect not only educators' assumptions, knowledge, and actions but also the organizational environment around them.

For example, Williams and Woods (1997) argue that closing the achievement gap requires educators to reject the "deficit hypothesis" that is so often used to explain the low achievement of poor children. Acting on this hypothesis causes schools to address only what students cannot do and to ignore the strengths that all children bring with them into the classroom. Consequently, poor children tend to experience a "bare bones" curriculum, devoid of the enrichment that accelerates the learning of their more economically advantaged peers. Williams and Woods go on to suggest that professional development should challenge the assumptions that support the deficit hypothesis, provide educators with alternative research-based principles on which to base their practice, illustrate what these new understandings look like in action, and seek ways of reinforcing these new actions in day-to-day school operation (see also Williams & Newcombe, 1994). In this way, then, educators get the message that the content of professional development is both organizationally valuable and valued.

Visionary Leadership

Exemplary leadership, both its presence and absence, is a frequent explanation for why some organizations are successful and others are not (Cuban, 1988; Deal & Peterson, 1994; Sergiovanni, 1992). That finding is reinforced in our research. Strong leadership was an important component in promoting and maintaining schools where sizable numbers of teachers were willing and able to assume responsibility for student success.

Leadership, we found, had several dimensions in supporting such an approach. One was that it was a function suitable for both teachers and administrators. The impetus for "It's my job" at both schools may have come from the top, but team leaders and other key staff nurtured its growth throughout the respective faculties.

A second aspect of leadership in these schools was a willingness to fight for what people believed in, often in the face of outside pressures. For example, Ridgecrest steadfastly hung on to its teaching assistants, even as other schools cut back on their use to accommodate tight budgets. In a similar vein, even though Granite's district wanted all schools to reserve an exclusive time for extra reading instruction to improve test scores, the school retained its "reteaching and enrichment" period for students to "catch up" in all subjects, believing that this would better serve their students' long-term success in school.

Third, the schools adopted an entrepreneurial spirit to make sure they had the resources to support the activities they thought were essential to maintaining their demanding approach to working with students. Granite volunteered to take part in a major foundation's reform initiative to enhance teacher's formal professional development, and Ridgecrest tapped local corporate support to fund before- and after-school reading programs.

Fourth, school leaders were data-driven, engaging in regular and systematic analysis of student performance, disaggregated by gender and race, to make instructional and curriculum decisions. Particular emphasis was given to the test score gap between majority and minority students.

Fifth, while the schools felt that they should and could promote the success of all students even without parents' help, they felt strongly that parental involvement was unquestionably valuable to the enterprise. Granite carried out this belief via frequent communication with individual families, both written and verbal. In her inimitable fashion, the principal at Ridgecrest established the expectation that every single parent would attend, assist with, or arrange some school activity during the year—and placed the name of every parent who had been in the building during the year on a display in the school's lobby.

Finally, leaders in the schools celebrated their efforts and were not bashful about praising one another. There was a strong sense of a collective "we," and those who did not ascribe to the common values were encouraged to work elsewhere.

Congruent Organizational Structures

Teachers, assistants, and administrators will not be able to maintain the effort necessary for promoting success for all students without having organizational arrangements that sustain rather than drain energy. Schools simply have to come up with ways to ease educators' burdens. Several examples of these were already noted above: the teaching assistants and lunchtime meeting time for staff at Ridgecrest, the common team time at Granite, and the other regular opportunities for professional development at both schools.

Other devices were also present. For example, Granite endured its share of discipline problems. When these problems threatened instructional time too seriously, teachers were able to send students to an in-school suspension room. There, the students continued to work on all their classroom assignments, with the help of a teacher, so that they could catch up or stay caught up. The faculty's approval of the room, however, was not wedded to the program's taking difficult students out of the classroom so much as it was to the program's role in keeping these students on track with assignments. Thus discipline and instruction were both accomplished.

Fullan (1999) defines one of the major challenges of the change process as removing the incoherence among priorities, policies, programs, and practices. Both schools exemplified the power of integrating a common focus across all initiatives and programs, ensuring that these were complementary with, instead of contradictory to, one another. In general, the schools' success in adhering to rigorous and demanding expectations stemmed partially from the fact that the faculty rarely had to surmount organizational obstacles to doing their jobs. Thus energy could be reserved for students rather than adults.

Parent Participation

Both schools sought parental involvement, and as mentioned above, Ridgecrest had established a tradition that every parent would take part in some activity at school during the year. While the schools did not use the lack of parental involvement as a reason for student failure, they were neither blind to nor demeaning of the value that parents could add to students' success in school. Thus an emphasis on parents was not inconsistent with the educators' self-reliance in working with students effectively. Parents could make a difference to be sure, they felt, and the more parents that became involved, the more energy teachers would have to give extra help to some students and further enrichment to others. Therefore we would not want the teachers' insistence that they were responsible for student success to lead others to adopt a cavalier attitude toward parents' centrality to education.

Indeed, based on some of the discussion in Chapter 3, it appears that parents may in fact be more of an ally than educators recognize. At the least, parents voiced opinions about what they wanted to see at school that were remarkably consistent with what some teachers who espoused the "It's my job"/"No excuses" belief were trying to do in the schools. Parents wanted teachers who set consistently high expectations, provided equal opportunity for all students to learn and be challenged by those expectations, offered a variety of instructional experiences for students to engage interesting content, made sure that extra help was available for those who needed it, and worked to continually enhance lines of communication between families and schools. Perhaps understandably, given that much of what parents and teachers did with children was invisible to each other, the teachers in the low-income schools we studied thought that they valued education more than the parents did and the parents from these schools thought that they were a little more committed to the children's education than the teachers were. This suggests the potential for a powerful alliance, one that might direct rather than divert educational energy.

Complementary Policies

Analogous to the need for a school to support teachers in ensuring student success is the need for school districts to support schools. The two schools we highlighted had created their own identities within systems where there were no other schools like them. They consequently were working with only minimal system support. Their intense level of effort was hard to maintain, as it would be for any school facing contradictory demands for its attention and resources.

Unfortunately, at Granite, the principal's eventual retirement precipitated considerable turmoil when the superintendent's message to the new principal was that the school needed changes. The concern was that Granite did not "act like" the other junior highs in the district, and thus Granite's maverick status was a "hot" topic in district politics. The faculty's devotion to its "rules" and the new administrator's mandate to change them clashed violently, resulting in an early departure of the new principal and transfer requests from nearly three-fourths of the teachers—almost all of whom actually left at the end of the year. The denouement entailed many more complications, but the key point is that the school's operational idiosyncrasies made the eventual disruption to its progress predictable and inevitable.

Both Granite and Ridgecrest were examples of "whole-school reform" insofar as their efforts intentionally implicated all aspects of school life. However, their internal integration was not necessarily consistent with what was going on throughout their respective districts. Thus one could not label the schools good examples of "systemic" reform. Actually, Granite illustrated the downside of poor reform alignment within the district, and we worry about Ridgecrest's future, especially should its principal leave.

We are not arguing against school-based flexibility and decision making. Differing contextual circumstances make the need for those features both obvious and sensible. What we are saying is that making a commitment to educating all children successfully is too demanding if educators have to surmount organizational, political, and economic obstacles while trying to serve children well. Therefore we are saying that districts must establish educating all children well as a central value and devise operational priorities, programs, practices, and policies that reinforce that value.

We should take this statement a step further. As we have shown, slogans such as "All children can succeed" and "Educate all children well" are subject to multiple interpretations. Almost any step a district might take could therefore be justified under the guises of these slogans. For example, a school or district could seek to improve the achievement of students who traditionally have performed poorly in school and rightfully label this goal as consistent with promoting success for all. However, if these students improve at the same or lower rates than other more traditionally successful students, then nothing will have been accomplished in terms of closing the performance gap among various groups of students. So districts could become better aligned organizationally without actually benefiting poor students educationally. We therefore argue that the central task around which districts with diverse students should establish complementary policies is closing the performance gap among its students.

Granite and Ridgecrest did so, and both evidenced considerable success. Our admonition is that for such success to be maintained, and for all children to flourish, then this goal must become districtwide, statewide, and nationwide.

CONCLUSION

Just as we warned the reader about the danger of listing practices teachers used to make sure that no students slipped through the cracks in their classroom floors, so, too, we disclaim the magic of the above avenues. Individual actions should not be the focal point so much as the assumption behind the action, and that assumption, according to the educators we have presented in this book, is that educators must assume the responsibility for making sure that all students succeed. Without this assumption, the actions become ritualistic—symbolic of aspiration perhaps, but devoid of substance.

For example, *Promising Results, Continuing Challenges* (U.S. Department of Education, 1999)—the final report from the national assessment of the Title I program—states that student achievement in this country has risen slowly but steadily since 1992. Heartened by this development on the National Assessment of Educational Progress (NAEP), the report concludes that American education needs to "stay the course"—with the "course" consisting primarily of standards, reduced class size, greater school and district accountability, and heightened parental involvement.

We do not quarrel with the strategies the report recommends, but rather with the assumption that they may be sufficient for improving the achievement of all children. To do that, we maintain, educators must infuse any promising educational practice with the steadfast belief that there are no excuses for student failure. For too long student failure has been rationalized: "These students just don't try," "What do you expect given what these kids go home to," or "They lack so much when the come to my class." Such excuses place the source of achievement differences outside of the school's influence and ensure that the differences will remain. Stated positively, what separates classrooms and schools where the achievement gap has been significantly reduced from those where it persists are educators who assert that "All children can succeed in school, *and it is our job to make sure that they do.*"

Educators we observed and talked with who worked in schools that had ameliorated group differences in achievement refused to allow either home situations or student motivation to serve as reasons why students failed. Instead, they expected and enabled each student to complete his or her work successfully and, quite simply, "nagged" the students until they did. They made sure everyone understood assignments and concepts and offered all the extra help students required. But enacting such strategies alone was not the hallmark of their approach. The actions had to be infused with the attitude that educators are responsible for student success.

Our concern is that devoting too much attention to specific "research-based" practices that generally target low-performing students will falsely comfort people, giving the appearance of bold action without actually threatening underlying assumptions about what "success for all" really means or requires us to do. Based on our research, we feel that there are some notable educators out there who are well ahead of the educational reform parade. They live achievement gaps and strive to close them. They believe all children can succeed if given the opportunity. For them, "It's my job" means doing any and every thing to ensure success. No wishing for more involved parents. No bemoaning the lack of eager children. No settling for a 5% increase in the overall number of children reaching a certain proficiency level. To be sure, they value interested parents, enthusiastic students, and higher test scores, but the absence of the first two and the attainment of the latter are not acceptable reasons for failing to educate every single child.

While in principle many policy makers and educators might regard such teachers as admirable, we have found few—other than in an occasional classroom within a school, school within a district, or office in a state building—who felt it was realistic. Fortunately for the students in these pockets of success, the adults who work with them never think this way. It is incumbent on adults in positions of influence in education to improve the chances for more children who traditionally have not done well in school to come into contact with educators who know how to close achievement gaps.

Thus, for example, introducing standards, reduced class sizes, and better means of accountability into the reform equation must arm educators with (1) the knowledge and the skills to use these developments to benefit students who have not succeeded in school and (2) the devout belief that these same students can learn challenging material. Local, state, and federal educational policies must explicitly support not only staying the course with effective strategies but also confronting the belief systems of educators so that they know and appreciate the power of denying students the option of failure. Therefore federal dollars should nurture professional development that promotes both "It's my job"/"No excuses" actions *and* attitudes and research that provides a rock-solid foundation for this endeavor. It is unacceptable to wait several generations while the gap closes and, in the interim, to doom numerous children to being perpetually unprepared for the future.

Parent Involvement Survey Items for Each Standard

(A) Parent Involvement

Communicating: Communicating between home and school is regular, two-way, and meaningful.

a) I go to school to talk with my child's teacher(s).
b) I visit my child's classroom(s) for special events.
c) I read school information brought home to me by my child.

Volunteering: Parents are welcome in the school, and their support and assistance are sought.

d) I assist the teacher(s) in classroom instruction.
e) I volunteer to work in the school library.
f) I assist the teacher(s) with paperwork.

Student Learning at Home: Parents play an integral role in assisting student learning.

g) I help my child prepare for tests.
h) I help my child plan time for homework.
i) I work with my child on learning activities in addition to what is required by school.

School Decision Making and Advocacy: Parents are full partners in the decisions that affect children and families.

j) I serve on PTA/PTO committees.
k) I serve on committees in my child's school (other than PTA/PTO).
l) I serve on local board of education committees.

Parenting: Parenting skills are promoted and supported.

    m) I ask my child questions about his or her day at school.
    n) I talk to my child about the importance of schooling.
    o) I talk to my child about educational possibilities beyond high school.

Collaborating with Community: Community resources are used to strengthen schools, families, and student learning.

    p) I encourage my child to participate in clubs or sports after school.
    q) I encourage my child to volunteer for community service through the school.
    r) I take my child to special places or events in the community.

(B) School Support for Parent Involvement

Communicating: Communicating between home and school is regular, two-way, and meaningful.

    a) My child's teacher has parent–teacher conferences with me.
    b) My child's teacher sends home timely notices about school events.
    c) My child's teacher makes telephone calls to me.

Volunteering: Parents are welcome in the school, and their support and assistance are sought.

    d) My child's school invites me to volunteer.
    e) My child's school offers training to volunteers.

Student Learning at Home: Parents play an integral role in assisting student learning.

    f) My child's teacher tells me what skills my child needs to learn.
    g) My child's teacher explains how to check my child's homework.
    h) My child's teacher assigns homework that requires my child to talk with me about things learned in class.

School Decision Making and Advocacy: Parents are full partners in the decisions that affect children and families.

    i) My child's school provides opportunities for me to communicate with them.

    j) My child's school invites me to be part of school committees.

    k) My child's school provides timely information on important school events.

Parenting: Parenting skills are promoted and supported.

    l)   My child's school offers parent education programs.

    m) My child's school makes parenting information available.

Collaborating with Community: Community resources are used to strengthen schools, families, and student learning.

    n) My child's school provides information to me on community services and activities.

    o) My child's school involves my child in community activities.

    p) My child's school involves community members in school activities.

References

Blacks battle achievement gap. (2000, December 31). *Washington Post*, p. C1.

Carter, C. (1999). *No excuses: Seven principals of low-income schools who set the standard for high achievement.* Washington, DC: The Heritage Foundation.

Consortium for Policy Research in Education (CPRE) et al. (1997). *A first-year evaluation report of Children Achieving: Philadelphia's education reform.* Philadelphia: Author.

Corbett, H. D., & Wilson, B. L. (1998). Scaling within rather than scaling up: Implications from students' experiences in reforming urban middle schools. *The Urban Review, 30*(4), 261–293.

Cuban, L. (1988). *The managerial imperative and the practice of leadership in schools.* Albany: State University of New York Press.

Darling-Hammond, L. (1997). *The right to learn: A blueprint for creating schools that work.* San Francisco: Jossey-Bass.

Deal, T. (1985). The symbolism of effective schools. *Elementary School Journal, 83* (3), 601–620.

Deal, T. E., & Peterson, K. D. (1994). *The leadership paradox: Balancing logic and artistry in schools.* San Francisco: Jossey-Bass.

Deschenes, S., Tyack, D., & Cuban, L. (2001). Mismatch: Historical perspectives on schools and students who don't fit them. *Teachers College Record, 103* (4), 525–547.

Epstein, J. L. (1995). School/family/community partnerships: Caring for the children we share. *Phi Delta Kappan, 76*, 701–712.

Fix the flaws in school reform [Editorial]. (2001, June 16). *New York Times*, p. A14.

Fullan, M. (1999). *Change forces: The sequel.* New York: Falmer.

Gardner, H. (1983). *Frames of mind: The theory of multiple intelligences.* New York: Basic Books.

Gordon, E. W. (2000). Bridging the minority achievement gap. *Principal, 79*(5), 20–23.

Harwell, M., D'Amico, L., Stein, M., & Gattie, G. (2000). *The effects of teachers' professional development on student achievement in Community School District #2.* Paper presented at the annual meeting of the American Educational Research Association, New Orleans.

Haycock, K. (2001). Closing the achievement gap. *Educational Leadership, 58*(6), 6–11.

Hoff, D. J. (2000). Gap widens between Black and White students on NAEP. *Education Week, 20*(1), 6–7.

Hedges, L., & Howell, A. (1999). Changes in the Black–White gap in achievement test scores. *Sociology of Education, 72*(2), 111–135.

Jencks, C., & Phillips, M. (1998). *The Black-White test score gap.* Washington, DC: Brookings Institution Press.

Knapp, M., Shields, P., & Turnbull, B. (1995). Academic challenge in high-poverty classrooms. *Phi Delta Kappan, 76,* 770–776.

Ladson-Billings, G. (1990). Culturally relevant teaching: Effective instruction for Black students. *The College Board Review, 155,* 20–25.

Ladson-Billings, G. (1994). *The dreamkeepers: Successful teachers of African American children.* San Francisco: Jossey-Bass.

Lipman, P. (1998). *Race, class, and power in school restructuring.* Albany: State University of New York Press.

McKenzie Group. (1999). *Student achievement and reform trends in 13 urban districts.* Washington, DC: Author.

Mezzacappa, D. (2001). A multipronged attack on a nagging problem. *Philadelphia Inquirer,* June 21, A1,6.

Molnar, A., Smith, P., & Zahorik, J. (1999). *Evaluation results of the student achievement guarantee in education (SAGE) program.* Madison: School of Education, University of Wisconsin.

Navarro, M., & Natalico, D. (1999). Closing the achievement gap in El Paso: A collaboration for K–16 renewal. *Phi Delta Kappan, 80*(8), 597–601.

Nieto, S. (1996). *Affirming diversity: The sociopolitical context of multicultural education.* White Plains, NY: Longman.

Prawat, R. (1993). The value of ideas: Problems versus possibilities in learning. *Educational Researcher, 22*(6), 5–16.

Roach, R. (2001). In the academic and think tank world, pondering achievement-gap remedies takes center stage. *Black Issues in Higher Education, 18*(1), 26–27.

Roscigno, V., & Ainsworth-Darnell, J. (1999). Race, cultural capital, and educational resources: Persistent inequalities and achievement returns. *Sociology of Education, 72*(3), 158–178.

Rothstein, R. (2000). *Improving educational achievement. A volume exploring the role of investments in schools and other supports and services for families and communities.* Washington, DC: Center of Education Policy.

San Miguel, T., Garza, R, & Gibbs, W. (2000, April). *Pre-kindergarten–16 educational accountability system: The Lone Star state's response and is anyone listening?* Paper presented at the annual meeting of the American Educational Research Association, New Orleans.

Schools unveil effort to close achievement gap. (2001, June 7). *Seattle Times,* p. B5.

Sergiovanni, T. J. (1992). *Moral leadership: Getting to the heart of school improvement.* San Francisco: Jossey-Bass.

Study hits HUB on school race gap. (2001, May 23). *Boston Globe*, p. B1.

U.S. Department of Education. (1999). *Promising results, continuing challenges: The final report of the national assessment of Title I.* Washington, DC: Author.

Viadero, D. (2000). North Carolina launches broad assault on the achievement gap. *Education Week, 19*(35), 23.

Williams, B. (Ed.). (1996). *Closing the achievement gap: A vision for changing beliefs and practices.* Washington, DC: Association for Supervision and Curriculum Development.

Williams, B., & Newcombe, E. (1994). Building on the strengths of urban learners. *Educational Leadership, 51*(8), 75–78.

Williams, B., & Woods, M. (1997). Building on urban learners' experiences. *Educational Leadership, 54,* 29–32.

Wilson, B.L., & Corbett, H.D. (2001). *Listening to urban kids: School reform and the teachers they want.* Albany: State University of New York Press.

Wilson, E. (1971). *Sociology: Rules, roles, and relationships.* Homewood, IL: Dorsey Press.

Winfield, L. (1991). Resilience, schooling and development in African American youth: A conceptual framework. *Education and Urban Society, 24*(1), 5–14.

Index

ABI system, at Granite, 84–86, 92, 99, 101–3
Accountability
  and "all children can succeed" belief, 17, 18, 24, 147, 148, 149, 156, 157
  and "it's my job" belief, 18, 24, 157
  of staff/faculty, 109, 116
  of students, 17, 24
Achievement
  and "all children can succeed" belief, 2, 5, 8, 10–11, 12, 13, 27, 147–48, 151–52, 156, 157
  and complementary policies, 156
  and cultural-deficit argument, 3, 4
  educational research about, 3
  and ethnicity, 97, 132, 147
  Evans's views about, 79–80
  at Granite, 6, 97
  and "it's my job" belief, 2, 131, 132, 134, 137, 151–52, 156, 157
  national debate about, 3
  overview of, 1–5
  and professional development, 151–52
  responsibility for, 8
  at Ridgecrest, 6, 129
  and schools that work for all students, 10–11
  strategies to increase, 147–48
  and student motivation, 4
Ainsworth-Darnell, J., 5
"All children can succeed" belief
  as acceptable, valid statement of fact, 8, 12
  and accountability, 17, 18, 24, 156, 157
  and achievement, 2, 5, 8, 10–11, 12, 13, 27, 147–48, 151–52, 156, 157
  becoming a school where, 147–58
  and behavior of students, 1, 2, 19–24, 25

  commitment to, 2, 155
  and complementary policies, 150, 154–56
  and culture, 3, 4, 5, 151
  different meanings of, 1, 6, 8, 10, 12–28, 131–32, 155
  and discipline, 25, 26, 153
  and effort, 1, 2, 10, 12, 18, 19–24, 27, 153, 155
  and excellence, 10
  and expectations, 2, 17, 18, 19, 150–51, 154, 157
  at Granite, 1, 12, 16, 148, 149, 150, 151, 152, 153–54, 155, 156
  and help, 20, 24, 154, 157
  implementation of, 17
  importance of, 156–58
  and individual differences, 4, 5, 14–16, 21–24
  and instruction, 14, 151, 153, 154
  and "it's my job" belief, 1–2, 5, 9, 12, 13–19, 131–46, 149–58
  and leadership, 150, 152–53
  limitations to, 12, 13
  and optimism of educators, 3–4
  and organizational structure, 149, 150, 153–54
  overview of, 12–13, 27–28, 147–49
  and overview of study, 6, 7
  and parents/family, 1, 7, 8, 12, 16, 19, 24–28, 147, 148, 150, 153, 154, 156, 157
  and policies, 9
  and principal, 18, 153, 155
  and professional development, 148, 150–52, 153, 158
  qualifiers as to, 1, 2, 7, 8, 13, 19–27
  and responsibility, 4–5, 12, 13–24, 27, 148, 149–50, 156

About the Authors

Dick Corbett is an independent educational researcher. He spends his time studying and evaluating school reform initiatives, with a particular emphasis on low-income schools. He obtained his Ph.D. from the School of Education at the University of North Carolina–Chapel Hill, with an emphasis in the sociology of education. He has published his research in books for Teachers College Press, Ablex, and the State University of New York Press—the most recent of which, *Listening to Urban Kids: School Reform and the Teachers They Want* (with Bruce L. Wilson), appeared in 2001. He has written articles for such journals as *Educational Researcher*, *Phi Delta Kappan*, *Educational Leadership*, *Curriculum Inquiry*, *Urban Review*, and *Education Policy*. He also edits a book series on restructuring and school change for the State University of New York Press.

Belinda Williams is a cognitive psychologist who has spent nearly 30 years studying the academic disparities and educational experiences of students from diverse racial and cultural groups and socioeconomically disadvantaged communities. Williams is the author of numerous publications and the editor of the Association for Supervision and Curriculum Development's (ASCD) best-selling book *Closing the Achievement Gap: A Vision for Changing Beliefs and Practices*. She received her doctorate in psychology from Rutgers University. Her career in education includes 17 years of administrative experience in Head Start and urban schools and 6 years of research and development in the U.S. Department of Education Office of Education Research and Improvement (OERI) regional laboratory system, including Brown University. More recently, she was the Director for Research and Development for CHANGES, a research center at the University of Pennsylvania. Currently she is a consultant for the National Education Association (NEA), state departments, universities, associations, and school districts.

Bruce Wilson is an independent researcher. He is also an adjunct faculty member at Teachers College, Columbia University, where he teaches a course on research methods. His research interests are in school change, educational policy, and organizational analysis. His most recent research focuses on bringing the student voice to educational reform initiatives. Those interests are currently being pursued to evaluate the implementation of the Onward to Excellence program created by the Northwest Regional Educational Laboratory, to study reforming science education in middle schools through the efforts of the Penn Merck Collaborative for Science Education, to evaluate a statewide effort by the Mississippi Arts Commission to infuse the arts throughout the curriculum, to investigate implementation and sustainability issues for the Talent Development program at Johns Hopkins University, and to explore the factors promoting a comprehensive partnership of reform for middle school education in Michigan in a project supported by the W. K. Kellogg Foundation. His publications include *Listening to Urban Kids: School Reform and the Teachers They Want* (with H. Dickson Corbett), *Mandating Academic Excellence: High School Responses to State Curriculum Reform* (with Gretchen Rossman), *Testing, Reform, and Rebellion* (with H. Dickson Corbett), and *Successful Secondary Schools: Visions of Excellence in American Public Education* (with Thomas B. Corcoran). His academic training was at Stanford University, where he earned a Ph.D. in sociology of education.